THE BOOK
OF
MAHSATI GANJAVI

In the street of the winehouse, I am a... dervish;
from that barrel of wine give me... what I wish.
Child of a Sufi I am... but, no infidel, devilish:
I'm master of none, my own servant to punish.

THE BOOK OF MAHSATI GANJAVI

Translation & Introduction

Paul Smith

NEW HUMANITY BOOKS

BOOK HEAVEN
Booksellers & Publishers

Copyright © Paul Smith 2005, 2008, 2012, 2015, 2021

NEW HUMANITY BOOKS
BOOK HEAVEN
(Booksellers & Publishers for over 50 years)
47 Main Road Campbells Creek
Victoria 3451 Australia

For a complete list & details of our over 1200 titles go to amazon.com/author/smithpa

ISBN: 978-1507879726

Poetry/Mysticism/Sufism/Women's Studies/
Persian Poetry/Middle East/Persian History

CONTENTS

The Life & Times & Poetry of Mahsati Ganjavi... 7

The Form, Function & History of the *Ruba'i*... 15

Selected Bibliography... 40

Ruba'iyat... 43

Appendixes: 133

Mahsati and Amir Ahmad see each other for the first time (British Library Or.8755, f. 29v)

The Life and Times and Poetry of Mahsati Ganjavi

We know very little of Manisa Mahsati (mah... 'moon', sati... 'lady') Ganjavi's life except that she lived in Ganjeh where Sultan Sanjar reigned (1117-57) and as she was a poet, singer, musician and chess-player at his court she would have known Anvari and other poets there. It is said that her father was a theologian of the city of Khujand and she was born there in 1098 and that after her father's death she and her mother went to Ganjeh where they were finally given a room in a brothel.

She was a court, dervish and ribald poet (perhaps due to her accommodation as a child). She knew Nizami and is said to have been buried in his mausoleum, having died in 1185... although he did not pass away until 1209, 24 years later! She also knew Omar Khayyam, and like Omar composed mainly in the *ruba'i* form and must be considered to have helped revolutionize it. She did compose a few *qit'as* (fragments) such as the following that have come down to us...

Do you want to unite with me?
You hold onto a useless desire!
One cannot even dream of it...
why hold to this useless desire?

Where's breeze one can't access:

can anyone ever win one's desire?

And another…

Would to God that I was that one's thumb-stall,

so on his thumb I might pine away, beyond recall;

whenever he would be shooting that arrow of his

I'd make sure I would myself by it suffer… thrall.

And, when that one would fasten me, O so right,

from that one's lips to grab some kisses, I'd stall.

It is stated that Mahsati composed this poem while watching a Turkish boy shooting arrows. It happened that his thumb-stall over-turned and he fastened it with his teeth.

She was also a great *ghazal* poet but few have come down to us. Alireza Korangy Isfahani (see bibliography) states: 'Mahasti Ganjavi is without a doubt one of the greatest *ghazal* poets of the twelfth century… her flow of ideas is very much akin to the kind of composition we find in the *ghazals* of Hafiz and Sa'di.'

A rare example of one of her *ghazals*…

With this sorrowful heart of mine, in tears constantly, I am;

like the flute, used to my own moaning its easy to see, I am.

Other than my two old companions, agony and affliction…

I've no other as a friend in this place where inevitably I am.

Who am I? A madwoman whose soul and heart wants pain

and thinks that death will my ultimate comfort be... I am.
At companions' feet I'm candle burning... I burn, so I live:
beyond that flame that flickers, my last days to see, I am.
Like that bubble I am that all of its life was able to survive
because like it knowing my foundation is water only, I am.
I'm a rosebud withered away that in spring lost its beauty:
my youth's a rose blown away by the wind, a memory I am.
It's only for death that to the Almighty I am praying often:
this is the only thing that looking forward to happily, I am.
For Mahasti no candle like a companion has been found...
would anyone come and mourn me when dead finally I am?

She was a strong influence on perhaps Persia's greatest female poet Jahan Khatun of Shiraz and Persia's greatest satirist Obeyd Zakani. She was famous and also infamous for her liberated behaviour. She is said to have had many affairs, also with the sultan who found her of interest when after he was about to mount his horse discovered a sudden fall of snow had covered the field and she composed for him the following *ruba'i* on the spot...

For you... Heaven has saddled Fortune's steed
O sultan... and chosen you from all who lead:
now it spreads a silver sheet upon the ground,
steed's gold-shod hooves... mud won't impede.

'Attar, in his masterpiece epic poem of mystical stories of desperate lovers of God, the *Ilahi-nama (Book of God)* that influenced Maulana Rumi to compose his epic *Masnavi* tells the story of her and Sultan Sanjar…

Mahsati the female poet, who was essentially pure, was a favourite of Sanjar…

and even though her face was not moonlike, still the king was very fond of her.

She was in the Radkan meadow one night when Khusrau-like Sanjar retired,

and Mahsati left the king and towards her own tent she then went, to bed.

Now, Sultan Sanjar had a slave, a winebringer perfect in charm and beauty,

and he would often enjoy both of these qualities, that in that one he did see.

Like a hundred others he loved Mahsati's rival, handsome as is the moon:

Sanjar woke up! Not seeing him he went looking for that ruby-lipped one.

Throwing on a nightgown and in anger taking up a sword of Indian make *he entered his tent to find Mahsati beside him, lovingly... in give and take.*

She kept singing these words as she was playing the haunting melody:

"I'll embrace you beside the meadow, although tonight with another I'll be!"

Seeing the situation, Sanjar... remembering her words, to himself said this:

"If I rush in with sword I'll scare them to death and both I'll terribly miss!"

Embarrassed, he finally rushed off and went immediately into his own tent,

and after ten days had passed he prepared a great feast, an illuminating event!

Before Sultan Sanjar, Mahsati played her harp, in a very high-pitched sound...

that winebringer was standing near, a cup in hand, eyes upon the ground.

Quoting the line he heard the other night Sanjar casually asked her to sing it:

when Mahsati heard the king she dropped harp from her lap where it did sit!

She started trembling like a leaf, she swooned, her senses caught in a snare;

the king went to sit by her pillow, sprinkled rosewater on her face and hair.

When finally she was conscious again... her fear returned of Sultan Sanjar,

after ten times fainting and recovering she still couldn't lose her great fear.

Then the king said, "If you're afraid of me, your life's safe, you're your enemy."

She said, "I don't fear that, but this: one night I practiced that line continually,

all night through I repeated it... sometimes I liked it, sometimes I did not:

now I am reminded of that night and the world is closing around me like a knot.

It seems that one night while I was doing this, you were secretly watching me:

if you seize me or send me away your heart will revolt and back... be calling me.

And even if you should go and be killing me while I am still a healthy woman...

all you would really be doing would be only freeing me from existence's prison!

The reason I'm so afraid is because that King Who is the world's supporter

is with me each moment of my life and sees every moment that I'm the doer!

And if God that Almighty King happens to confront me with all of my

secret thoughts of say... a hundred years, then what shall I do or say, or try?"

As God sees one always, both night and day; be happy, and smile while

like a candle, you are burning and do not breathe a single breath... while

you're not thanking Him... and do no not breathe a breath in forgetfulness:

if you try to thank Him you will receive reward from His Bountifulness.

She finally married (some say was the mistress of) a son of a preacher, the poet Taju'd-din Amir Ahmad and she found little satisfaction in their torrid relationship and so composed among others the following *ruba'i*...

I'm Mahsati and I'm most fair of those to be had:
I am famous for my beauty from Irak to Meshad.
Preacher's boy, you're nothing but useless... bad:
if I get no bread, meat or prick, I get really mad!
Her husband's reply was said to have been...
My prick does not always do what I tell it to:
it's not like your pussy... taking anyone's too!
Weaving a sack out of wool any idiot can do...
but, wind will heighten a tower... is that true?

Her purported love affairs are told in the works of Jauhari of Bukhara.

After nearly 900 years, Mahsati is highly respected for her courageous poetry that condemned religious fanaticism and prejudices, hypocrisy and dogmas.

In the city of Ganjeh in Azerbaijan, a street and a school, an academic institution, a museum and others have been named after her. A monument to her was erected in Ganjeh in 1980.

About 300 of Mahsati's *ruba'is* have survived. This edition of 250 is the largest in English in the correct form.

The Form, Function & History of the *Ruba'i*

Most scholars of Persian Poetry agree that the *ruba'i* is the most ancient Persian poetic form that is original to this language. All other classical forms including the *ghazal, qasida, masnavi* etc., they say originated in Arabic literature and the metres employed in them were in Arabic poetry in the beginning. The *ruba'i* is a poem of four lines in which usually the first, second and fourth lines rhyme and sometimes with the *radif* (refrain) after the rhyme words... sometimes all four rhyme. It is composed in metres called *'ruba'i'* metres. Each *ruba'i* is a separate poem in itself and should not be regarded as a part of a long poem as was created by FitzGerald when he translated those he attributed to Omar Khayyam (only 10% of Omar's poems were by him).

The *ruba'i* (as its name implies) is two couplets *(beyts)* in length, or four lines *(misra)* as stated above. The *ruba'i* is different in metre from all those used in Arabic poetry that preceded it. How was this metre invented? The accepted story of Rudaki (d. 941 A.D.) creating this new *metre* of the *hazaj* group which is essential to the *ruba'i* is as follows: one New Year's Festival he happened to be strolling in a garden where some children played with nuts and one threw a walnut along a groove in a stick and it jumped out then rolled back again creating a sound and the children shouted with delight in imitation, *'Ghaltan ghaltan hami ravad ta bun-i gau,' [Ball, ball, surprising hills… to end of a brave try]*. Rudaki immediately recognised in the line's metre a new invention and by the repetition four times of the *rhyme* he had quickly created the *ruba'i*… and is considered the first master of this form and the father of classical Persian Poetry.

Shams-e Qais writing two hundred years later about this moment of poetic history and the effect of this new form on the population said the following… "This new poetic form fascinated all classes, rich and poor, ascetic and drunken outsider *[rend]*, all wanted to participate in it… the sinful and the good both loved it; those who were so ignorant they couldn't make out the difference between poetry and prose began to dance to it; those with dead hearts who couldn't tell the difference between a donkey braying and reed's wailing and were a thousand miles away from listening to a lute's strumming, offered up their souls for a *ruba'i*. Many a young girl cloistered away, out of passion for the song of a *ruba'i* broke down the doors and their chastity's walls; many matrons from love for a *ruba'i* let loose the braids of their self-restraint."

The *ruba'i* should be eloquent, spontaneous and ingenious. In the *ruba'i* the first three lines serve as an introduction to the fourth that should be sublime, subtle or pithy and clever. As can be seen from the quote by Shams-e Qais above the *ruba'i* immediately appealed to all levels of society and has done so ever since. The nobility and royalty enjoyed those in praise of them and the commoner enjoyed the short, simple homilies... the ascetic and mystic could think upon epigrams of deep religious fervour and wisdom; the reprobates enjoyed the subtle and amusing satires and obscenities... and for everyone, especially the cloistered girls and old maids, many erotic and beautiful love poems to satisfy any passionate heart.

Every major and most minor poet of Persia composed at some times in the *ruba'i* form. I will now attempt a short history of the finest exponents and innovators of this form... many of course would have had an influence on Mahsati, (with a brief look at what Mahsati brought to this form). A fuller exploration of this subject, with a much greater selection of poems and sources can be discovered in my... *The Ruba'iyat: A World Anthology.*

HANZALAH (Mid. 9th century). It seems that Hanzalah of Baghis (a district north-west of Herat) was inspired by Abbas of Merv's example and began to compose poems in Persian. 'Awfi says of his poetry, 'the graceful flow of his expression is like the water of Paradise and his couplets are fresh like cool wine and likeable like the north wind'. His poems became so popular that his were probably the first to be collected into a *Divan*, but unfortunately like many of these early poets, only a few fragments remain. In what some scholars say is the first *ruba'i* (but of a different metre than that discovered by Rudaki and in which most *ruba'is* were composed after that)... Hanzalah warns his sweetheart it is futile to throw rue-seed on fire to avoid the influence of the evil eye, an old superstition.

> *Though my sweetheart rue-seed on fire threw*
> *so that from the evil eye no hurt would accrue:*
> *what is the use of fire and rue-seed to one whose face is like fire... mole, like seed of rue?*

MANSUR AL-HALLAJ (859-922). Mansur al-Hallaj was a Perfect Master and a poet who like Jahan was born in or near Shiraz, Persia... a writer and teacher of Sufism most famous for his self-proclaimed divinity in his poetry and for his execution for heresy at the hands of the Abbasid rulers. Although Hallaj was born in Persia and was of Persian descent, he wrote all of his works in Arabic. He possibly met Rudaki (to follow).

He married and made a pilgrimage to Mecca, stayed for one year, facing the mosque, in fasting and total silence. After his stay at the city, he traveled extensively and wrote and taught along the way. He traveled as far as India and Central Asia gaining many followers, many of whom accompanied him on his second and third trips to Mecca. After this period of travel, he settled down in the capital of Baghdad.

During his early lifetime he was a disciple of Junaid and Amr al-Makki, but was later rejected by them both. Among other Sufis, Hallaj was an anomaly. Many Sufi masters felt that it was inappropriate to share his inner experiences with the masses, yet Mansur Hallaj openly did so in his writings and through his teachings. He began to make enemies, and the rulers saw him as a threat. This was exacerbated by times when he would fall into trances that he attributed to being in the presence of God. During one of these trances, he would utter *Anal-Haqq* literally meaning,

"I am the Absolute Truth", which was taken to mean that he was claiming to be God. In another controversial statement, Hallaj claimed: "There is nothing wrapped in my turban but God," and he would point to his cloak and say, "There is nothing inside my cloak except God."

These utterances led him to a long trial, and subsequent imprisonment for eleven years in a Baghdad prison. In the end, he was tortured and publicly crucified (in some accounts he was beheaded and his hands and feet were cut off) by the Abbasid rulers for what they deemed 'theological error threatening the security of the state.' Many accounts tell of Hallaj's calm demeanor even while he was being tortured, and indicate that he forgave those who had executed him. He was executed on March 26, 922. It is said that while he was savagely tortured before he was killed he kept calling out: *"Anal Haqq!"* It is also reported that after his body was burnt and the ashes thrown into the Tigris River they spelt out the words *"Anal Haqq!"* His influence on all Sufis, be they poets or not, who have come after him, cannot be overestimated.

I'm the One I love, the One I love is
me,
we are two spirits that live... in one

body.
If you see me, then... you see that One,
and, if you see that One... both, you see.

A secret, hidden for a long time, is told to
you...
from the dark of night, from you, a day dawns
too:
the veil of the heart over its secret mystery is
you,
it would never have been sealed if not for you,
too.

*

SHIBLI (d.946). A pupil and disciple of Junaid of Baghdad and one who had met Mansur Hallaj, Al-Shibli is one of the famous Sufis. He was originally from Khurasan. In the book *Rawdat al-jannat,* and in other biographies, many mystical poems and sayings have been recorded of him. Ansari has said: "The first person to speak in symbols was Dhu al-Nun of Egypt. Then came Junaid and he systematized this science, extended it, and wrote books on it. Al-Shibli, in his turn, took it to the pulpit." He died in 846 at the age of 87. He composed his poems in Arabic.

I will put upon me a fine robe of patience…
keeping awake at night for longer makes sense.
I am not yet willing to be patient completely…
a bit at a time soul I'll try bring, to my defence.

*

ABU SHAKUR (b. 915). Abu Shakur of Balkhi appeared before both Shahid and Rudaki and is said to have from both of them 'carried off the ball of excellence'. He was a bi-lingual poet and the earliest poet to use the *mutakarib* metre in his epic *masnavi Afarin-Nama* composed in 948. He claimed he couldn't speak a lie to his beloved, because that 'would tie his neck into a yoke'. His style is simple, some of his poems are like jingles, or child-like. Perhaps he was the originator of the *ruba'i* or perhaps he too like Shahid (to follow) got the *ruba'i* metre off Rudaki (to follow)… they all being alive at the same time.

From stabs of grief for you, I am laid low;
bowed down by separation's burden, I go.
I washed hands of your wiles and tricks…
none had moods, whims like yours I know.

*

SHAHID (d. 937). Shahid of Balkh was mourned in a poem by his friend the great Rudaki (next). He was said to be 'of excellent mind, a spirited conversationalist, with high opinions and a scholar'. The melancholy that is in some of his poems meant that he was eventually called, 'the pessimist of the century'. He was said to be one of the great philosophers of his time. In the following *ruba'i* probably composed after those of his friend Rudaki he laments over the ruins of Tus in Khurasan that had been devastated by invading hordes.

Last night by the ruins of Tus I passed

by,

seeing owl sitting in place of peacock saw

I.

I asked, "What do you know of these ruins?"

It answered, "News is, O no... I could cry!"

*

RUDAKI was born in the village of Rudak (hence his pen-name or *takhallus)* in Transoxania in 858 A.D. The historian 'Awfi says that Rudaki was blind from birth but other historians of the time disagree with him asking how one could create such images of nature if he did not at one time see. Others say that a ruler later in his life held red-hot iron rods before his eyes and blinded him when he refused to compose poetry for him.

First a wandering 'dervish' poet he later served at the court of the Samanids of Bokhara. Rudaki was so intelligent and like Hafiz of Shiraz (1320-1392) blessed with such a fine memory that by the age of eight he had memorized all of the *Koran.* He is said to have had a happy childhood spending much of his time listening to stories and songs and learning about his people's ways and aspirations. He began to compose poems expressing their desires and his own. He had a beautiful voice and was a fine musician and because of this he mixed freely with other minstrels and with musicians and dancers. His lute teacher was the famous Bakhtiar and he eventually excelled his master. He travelled around the Tajikistan highlands with his master, singing and creating songs. When Bakhtiar died and left him his famous lute he continued wandering and singing until his fame reached the capital... Bokhara.

Nasr ibn Ahmad summoned him to his court and he prospered there amassing great wealth. He had 200 slaves in his retinue... and 400 camels carried his belongings when he travelled. He was commissioned and paid 40,000 *dirhams* to translate *Kalila and Dimna* (a collection of fables originating in India and translated into Arabic in 750) into Persian verse (*masnavi*... rhyming couplets). This work, plus most of the reported 1,300,000 couplets (some say 130,000) that he composed (his *Divan*) have not survived the ravages of time. There remain only 1000 couplets... 52 *kasidas, ghazals* and *ruba'is.* Of his epic masterpieces we have nothing beyond a few lines. In 937 he fell out of favour at court (perhaps he was blinded at this time) after the death of the prime-minister who had supported him. His life ended in abject poverty, forgotten by the world at that time. Rudaki died in Rudak in 941. His poetry is about the passage of time, old age, death, fortune's fickleness, importance of the matters of the heart, the need to be happy. Although he praised kings, nobles and heroes... his greatest love was knowledge and experience.

With what one has, be satisfied,
live freely:
by any formality do not be tied...
live freely!
Don't pity self if others seem richer:
many more are by fortune tried.
Live, freely!

No sun blazes in this world, more than the face
of Yours!
No light graces this world more than that grace
of Yours!
Let not a one ever be as spoiled as I am by You,
each day may not any face seen, be even a trace
of Yours!

*

FIRDAUSI (941-1021). Next, in our tracing of the *ruba'i* through the words of Persia's greatest exponents of the poetic arts, we come to Iran's national poet, known throughout the land and many others as the creator of the 60,000 couplets he called 'Book of Kings' or *Shah-nama*. He was a lot less prolific than Iran's previous other 'immortal', Rudaki, and occasionally gave up the *masnavi* form of different rhyming couplets and composed in the *ruba'i* form. Born the year that Rudaki died, in Tus, the ancient city in Khorasan, Abdul Qasim Mansur would use the *takhallus* or pen-name of Firdousi (Paradise) calling himself that after the name of a garden his father looked after... being a small but proud landowner. His *Shah-nama* took thirty years to complete and he was only paid 20,000 *dirhams* of the 50,000 promised to him by Sultan Mahmud and he bitterly wrote satires on that ruler in his old age. The following *ruba'i* was possibly composed about the Sultan in earlier, happier times...

> *Showing his servants much kindness*
> *last night,*
> *he acted like a human being, no less,*
> *last night.*
> *Faults forgiving, taking arm, laughing*
> *loudly, it... around his neck he did press*
> *last night.*

*

ABU SAID (948-1049) was the famous Perfect Master who composed over 400 *ruba'is*. He is considered to be one of the founders of Sufi poetry and was a major influence on the *ruba'i* and most poets that followed, especially Sana'i, Attar and Rumi and Hafiz.

>This body was all tears that were by my eyes
>shed,
>in this love for You one must have no form or
>head.
>What is this love? Not one trace of me stays!
>Who is the lover, ever since I've become... the
>Beloved?

>Instead of sleep there is much water
>in these eyes,
>I'm so impatient to have You... here,
>in these eyes:
>I'm told: sleep, in dreams I'll see You;
>but, they don't know no sleep's there,
>in my eyes.

*

IBN SINA (981-1037). Abu 'Ali Ibn Sina (or as he is called in the west... Avicenna) born some forty years after Firdousi in Bukhara died about twenty-five years after him, living only for fifty-six years even though he was one of the greatest creative exponents of the great arts of *Koranic* knowledge, arithmetic and algebra, medicine, surgery and philosophy and wrote poems in Arabic and Persian so much so that that some *ruba'is* he composed were later to be ascribed to Omar Khayyam. He was hounded as a heretic and worse, but all the known world is still trying to catch up to what he discovered. His *kasida* on the human soul is considered one of the greatest Persian poems of all time. His *ruba'is* are some of the most honest and direct of all time.

> *I was asked by a person, "Tell me, what is*
> *the Absolute?"*
> *Beyond description and imaginable bliss...*
> *the Absolute!*
> *One cannot speak of why It is or what It is:*
> *only the Absolute can really say, "This... is*
> *the Absolute!"*

*

BABA TAHIR ('The Naked')... approx. 990-1065, was a great God-intoxicated soul *(mast)* and possibly a *Qutub* (Perfect Master) who composed about 120 known *ruba'i* in a simpler metre than the usual *'hazaj'* metre. His simple, mystical poems that he would sing while wandering naked throughout the land had a profound influence on Sufis and dervishes and other *ruba'i* composers, especially Abu Said.

*I am a kalandar... a drunken outsider, a vagabond,
on such a one like me life has no ties, no bond:
during day I wander aimlessly... at night my pillow's a stone... my lamp the moon beyond.*

BABA KUHI... d.1051. A Perfect Master poet who like Jahan lived in the fabled city of Shiraz. His tomb is on a hill outside that city and it was at that tomb that the greatest of all Persian mystical love poets Hafiz kept vigil for forty nights and received from this Master the gift of poetry, immortality and 'his heart's delight'.

The work isn't finished without love's fire,
my dear:
heart isn't perfect unless consumed entire,
my dear.
Burn day and night like moth and candle:
day is Beloved's face, night hair to admire,
my dear.

Ever since the First Day as drunken lover
I've come
with the winecup in hand... until forever,
I've come.
I am lover, drunkard, worshipper of wine:
do not blame me for like this I was before
I've come.

ANSARI... 1006-1089. The great mystical poet Khwaja Abdullah Ansari who passed from this world 1089 in Herat is most known for his biographical dictionary on saints and masters and his much loved collection of inspiring prayers, the *Munajat*. His *ruba'is* appear throughout his works.

From loving you, without soul and heart
I've become,
twisted like your curls, that play a part,
I've become.
No, a mistake: now that by love's power
I'm beyond both worlds, the Sweetheart
I've become.

*

AL-GHAZZALI (1058-1112). Mohammad al-Ghazzali the famous theologian was born in Tus in 1058 and after his many extraordinary expositions on the knowledge of the spiritual path, Islamic philosophy was never the same. He has been called 'The Proof of Islam' and the learned Suyuti once said of him, "If there could have been another prophet after Mohammed it would surely have been al-Ghazzali!" His *Alchemy of Happiness* is of course his most popular work but he was also a composer of a number of fine *ruba'is*.

O Being's Essence… is there one being
You are not in?
You are no place, but there is no thing…

You are not in?
O You, not needing direction or place...
what, is Your Place? Is a place missing,
You are not in?

*

OMAR KHAYYAM... (died 1132). Of the 1000 or so *ruba'is* attributed to him only about ten percent are now considered to be his. More famous in Iran as an astronomer and mathematician his nihilistic and hedonistic philosophy in his *ruba'is* meant that his poems were never really popular in his homeland.

Don't let your soul in sorrow's grasp be pressed,
don't let your days be filled... with vain unrest:
book, beloved's lips, meadow's edge don't give up... even if the earth folds you in its breast.

*

SANA'I... d. 1131. One of the most prolific and influential Sufi Master Poets of all time Sana'i composed many *ghazals, masnavis* and over 400 *ruba'is*. His long *masnavi* (rhyming couplets) mystical work *The Enclosed Garden of the Truth* is said to have had a profound influence on Rumi's composing his *Masnavi* and Sadi's his *Bustan* ('The Orchard').

> *Go to the winehouse, be a drunken lover*
> *only:*
> *there, wine and music and beloved order,*
> *only.*
> *Fill the large cup and before flagon of wine*
> *joyfully drink... speak sense to him or her*
> *only.*

*

MAHSATI (1098-1185). We know little of Mahsati Ganjavi's life except that she lived in Ganjeh where Sultan Sanjar reigned and as she was a poet at his court she would have known Anvari. She was a court, dervish and ribald poet. She knew Nizami (she is said to have been buried in his mausoleum) and Omar Khayyam... and like Omar composed only in the *ruba'i* form and must be considered not only a master of that form but also to have helped revolutionize it. She was an influence on perhaps Iran's greatest female poet Jahan Khatun of Shiraz and Iran's greatest satirist Obeyd Zakani. She was famous and also infamous for her liberated behaviour and is said to have had many affairs not only with the sultan who found her of interest when after he was about to mount his horse discovered a sudden fall of snow had covered the field and she composed for him the following *ruba'i* on the spot…

For you… Heaven has saddled Fortune's steed
O sultan… and chosen you from all who lead:
it spreads a silver sheet on the ground,
steed's gold-shod hooves… mud won't impede.

In the street of the Winehouse I am a dervish,
from that barrel of wine give me what I wish.
A child of a Sufi I am… but no infidel, devilish:

I'm master of none, my own servant to punish.

*

ANVARI (d. 1187). A court poet of the Seljik sultans. Jami composed a *ruba'i* where he names him along with Firdausi and Sadi as one of the 'three apostles' of Persian poetry. Mainly a court poet he was also an astrologer.

I spent many a night until morning wanting you…
many happy days kissing your lips I had, it's true:
now that you have gone, day and night I say,
"Day I meet beloved, let that night be happy too!"

NIZAMI (d. 1208). Another Master Poet who is most famous for his six books in *masnavi* form: *The Treasury of the Mysteries, Layla and Majnun, Khrosrau and Shirin, The Seven Portraits* and his two books on Alexander. He also composed a *Divan* of approximately 20,000 couplets in *ghazals* and *ruba'is*… tragically only 200 couplets survive. His influence on Attar, Rumi, Sadi, Hafiz and Jami and all others that followed was profound.

Wine is the best thing of all consumed by man,
find pure wine found in temple ruins if you can:
as the world's a ruined place with nowhere not ruined: be ruined, drunk, in the ruins O man!

*

RUZBIHAN... d. 1210. This Sufi Perfect Master of Shiraz is better known for his Spiritual Diary... *The Unveiling of Secrets*. He wrote mainly in Arabic and his *rubai's* are few of his works in Persian.

Searching for the cup of Jamshid the world I travelled:
I didn't rest a day... sleep never entered my head.
When Jamshid's cup I heard by my Master described,

that I myself was that world-seeing cup... I
realized.

*

ATTAR (d. 1230?). Farid ad-din Attar is the Perfect Master Poet who was the author of over forty books of poetry and prose including *The Conference of the Birds, The Book of God* (which he is said to have presented to Rumi when he met him) and *The Lives of the Saints*. Apart from his many books in *masnavi* form he also composed many hundreds of mystical *ghazals* and *ruba'is*. He also changed the evolution of the *ruba'i* form by composing a long Sufi epic, the *Mukhtar-nama,* where each of 2088 *ruba'is* is connected by subject matter which Fitzgerald attempted to do with those he attributed to Omar Khayyam.

Heart, since you drank spiritual knowledge's
wine,
keep lips closed... don't sell any secrets of the
Divine.
Don't boil like mountain spring in difficulties:
if you sit, silently, You will become Ocean, so
fine.

In love with that One's face is this soul

of mine...

also that One's talking... is heart, whole,

of mine.

Full of precious treasures... heart and soul

of mine:

what to do, for locked... is tongue and jowl

of mine.

A NOTE ON THIS TRANSLATION

In the Persian language there is no 'she' or 'he'... only *'oo'* or the person or object referred to... i.e. 'you' or 'that one'. Most translators wrongly either use 'he' or she' depending on their interpretations. I have not done this. Sometimes the poet is addressing the Divine Beloved (or Spiritual Master or *'Qutub'* in Sufi terminology) and sometimes an earthly beloved, so I make the judgment as to which and either capitalize or not, as in 'You' and 'you', 'that one' and 'that One'.

SELECTED BIBLIOGRAPHY

Divan-i Mahsati Ganjavi, Edited by Tahiri Sharab, Ibn Sina, Tehran, 1347 A.H.

The Ruba'iyat of Mahsati: Translation & Introduction by Paul Smith, New Humanity Books, 2009.

A Thousand Years of Persian Ruba'iya't by Reza Saberi. Ibex Publishers Maryland 2000. (Pages 158-170).

Princesses, Sufis, Dervishes, Martyrs & Feminists: Nine Great Women Poets of the East. Translations, Introduction & Notes by Paul Smith, New Humanity Books, Campbells Creek, 2012.

The Ruba'iyat: A World Anthology, Translation & Introduction by Paul Smith, New Humanity Books, 2009.

The Sufi & Dervish Ruba'iyat: An Anthology, Translation & Introduction by Paul Smith, New Humanity Books, 2009.

The Ilahi-nama or Book of God of Farid al-Din 'Attar Translated from the Persian by John Andrew Boyle, Manchester University Press, 1976 (Pages 218-20, 375).

Four Eminent Poetesses of Iran: by M. Ishaque. Iran Society, Calcutta, 1950. (Pages 9-28).

Development of the Ghazal and Khaqani's Contribution: A Study on the Development of Ghazal and a Literary Exegesis of a 12th c. Poetic Harbinger: A dissertation presented by Alireza Korangy Isfahani. Harvard University 2007. (UMI microform 3265145). (Pages 325 et al.)

Die schone Mahsati: Ein Beitrag zur Geschichte des persischen Vierzeilers. Vol 1. Fritz Meier, Wiesbaden 1963 (Pages 43-57).

Piercing Pearls: The Complete Anthology of Classical Persian Poetry: Volume One Translations & Introduction by Paul Smith, New Humanity Books, Campbell's Creek. 2008.

Suppressed Persian. An Anthology of Forbidden Literature. Paul Sprachman. Mazda Publications 1995. (Pages 1-5, 8, 61).

A Literary History of Persia Vol 1 From the Earliest Times to Firdawsi By Edward G. Browne. London 1902. (Page 344).

History of Iranian Literature by Jan Rypka et al. D. Reidel Publishing Company Holland. 1968 (Page 199).

Borrowed Ware: Medieval Persian Epigrams, Translated by Dick Davis. Mage Publishers, 1997. (Pages 105-107).

Le Luna e te perle (The moon and the pearls) Italian Translation of her poems by R. Bargigli, D. Meneghini, Ariel Pub. 1999.

Nozhat al-Majalas (Joy of Gatherings) A collection of 4100 ruba'is, 60 by Mahsati. Compiled by the poet Shirvani in the 13th c. Tehran, 1987.

Azerbaijanian Poetry, Classic, Modern, Traditional... Edited by Mirza Ibrahimov, Progress Publishers, Moscow, 1969. (Pages 43-47) Trans. by Gladys Evans).

Six Vowels & Twenty-three Consonants: An Anthology of Persian Poetry From Rudaki To Langroodi, Edited and translated bu Ali Alizadeh and John Kinsella, Arc Publications, Todmordon, 2012. (Pages 43-47).

Rubaiyat of Mahsati Ganjavi Text by Sugra Ibrahimgyzy (not printed) & Preface by her. Translation by Irina Zubanova, Baku 2014 (Terrible translation in very bad English... no text, approx. 60 ruba'is). Why bother?

Quarters (Ruba'iyat) of Mahsati Ganjavi by Nigar Rafibeyli & Kahil Yusifli, Leader Publishing House, Baku 2004, (In Azerbaijani) Hundreds of ruba'is. An interesting book! For reasonable English trans. Go to Archive.com

RUBA'IYAT...

To be a winehouse regular and a *kalandar,** a lover
too:
being in a gang of friendly *rends,** drunken outsider
too,
to be one who is infamous before creation… Creator
too:
is, than wearing any hypocrite's cloak… far better,
too.

**Note: Kalandars are lovers of God who have given up
attachment to desires and live only for God. The name comes
from a Master named Kalandar Yusuf. The word means 'pure gold.'
Kalandars are continually on the move and care nothing for their own
condition, as they are only concerned with praising God. *Rends are
drunken outsiders, reprobates, mad lovers.*

In the street of the winehouse, I am a… dervish;
from that barrel of wine give me… what I wish.
Child of a Sufi I am… but, no infidel, devilish:
I'm master of none, my own servant to punish.

Get up, come, my chamber I've made beautiful,
and for you I've spread carpet, O so wonderful!
Come; join me for *kebab* and wine I have made
from heart and eye, for you to eat… until full.

The bazaar of my heart with Your fair-trading
is happy,
with Your beautiful rook, chess of my longing
is happy.
In square of checkmate, You always place me:
O Soul, who with a checkmate, everlasting…
is happy?

You should not in vain rain tears from your eyes, I
believe:
this grief I have is enough, in heart you should not
grieve.
You are beloved, your occupation's not to weep…
I'm a desperate lover: let me work, let me my goal
achieve.

Ever since these eyes of mine did happen to see
your eyes;
sleep fled from my eyes, far from, unfortunately,
your eyes.
You, whose eyes the sight of all eyes make bright,
never did my eyes see others like their majesty…
your eyes.

From both these eyes, these tears, endlessly
are coming,
they, for you who cease to love... effortlessly
are coming.
Careful you've respect for these tears of mine,
for from this heart's *Kaaba*... caravans to me
are coming.

Prayer, when many gods are in the heart:
what good is it?
Antidote, after poison is far in the heart,
what good is it?
To display virtuousness after having a clean
garment over some dirty scar in the heart,
what good is it?

For you... Heaven has saddled Fortune's
steed
O sultan... and chosen you from all who
lead:
now it spreads a silver sheet on the ground,
steed's gold-shod hooves... mud won't
impede.

Unless Your hyacinth, ambergris is quickly
spreading,
morning breeze from bag... musk will not be
spreading.
If a hundred-year-old ascetic sees Your hand…
don't blame me if he asceticism is no longer
practicing.

May *rends* cheering be rending winehouse's air
constantly,*
and the fire from their cries catch onto skirts of
austerity.
May the Sufis' patched coats, blue woolen cloaks,
fall off to lie under the feet of all dreg-drainers,
immediately!

*Note: Rends are wanderers, profligates, drunkards, true lovers of God.

Drunkenly, your Turkish eyes are... waking
up:
from wine in wine-lovers, delirium is coming
up.
As you rise, allow your hair in air to dance...
from you sitting, a hundred riots are starting
up.

That one, smitten by your beauty,
has returned:
one, for union with you, thirsty...
has returned.
Clean cage, toss seeds of kindness:
this broken-winged bird you see...
has returned.

Since in the world of love my heart became a
king
it was freed from not believing and also from
believing.
I saw my lower self as obstacle on my path...
when I came out of it, my way for me was
opening.

My eyes are only ocean of tears…
sorrow:
my burden a mountain never bears:
sorrow.
Desiring friend… precious life passed:
I want companion… all there is, is
sorrow!

In the winehouse bowing before a beauty
is good,
praying over a goblet of wine, truthfully,
is good.
Not: worshipper showing off his rosary,
is good.
In winehouse, girdle of Magian to see…
is good.

Each moment pain to one needing
keeps coming
from you: cruelty to one suffering,
keeps coming.
In killing of lovers, do not try so hard:
careful, harm to you that's coming
keeps coming.

In the orchard last night I was moaning, grieving:
as I walked… tears over my body I kept shedding.
The red rose was appearing, her skirt was tearing,
and all her blouse with my tears she was spoiling.

When that one takes from off a victim, another
knife,
between sweet lips and teeth that one puts the
knife.
If that one holds it against victim's throat again,
the joy on that one's lips give to victim another
life.

When ruby-coloured tears from my eyes
keep dripping,
water from stone's heart and sky's eyes
keep dripping.
When they're from you cut off, my eyes
keep dripping:
from the cut, blood... obviously my eyes
keep dripping.

I am a drunk and of the drunkards...
a slave:
I'm far from ascetics and of libertines
a slave.
I'm of moment winebringer comes, saying...
"I can't, be free to join the drinkers!"
A slave.

Anyone who desires a love, that is... full of grace,
at midnight in blood soaks prayer-mat, any place.
Haven't you heard? The lovers have pitched love's
tent... beyond where seven heavens turn in space!

Does night know anything about how lovers are
suffering,
how from that goblet of calamity those lovers are
sipping:
how grief will be killing them, if the secret they're
hiding,
and if it they're revealing, the people them will be
killing.

A lover must go and risk one's life in love's way:
and, turn upside-down heart's peace, every day!
When one witnesses that Beloved is satisfied…
with suffering heart one dies, as one can't stay!

With your face your hair is in such harmony
I'm afraid I'll start blaspheming out of envy:
O graceful one… I'll bow to that breeze that
from your face takes your hair… completely!

This body of mine has a heart full of ecstasy
inside…
it also has soul with a thousand flames to see,
inside.
When day and night I'm longing for your face:
I have two eyes full of streams flowing freely,
inside!

All of those nights that in love with you I slept,
are gone!
You've left me and all what I told you to be kept,
are gone!
You were soul's friend… you were my heart's peace:
you disappeared and those tears that you wept,
are gone.

This affair of mine, beyond dry lips and wet eyes
did pass;
your cruel arrow through my heart and soul flies:
did pass.
To me fire of your love was like water in shallows…
but, when I stepped into it, it then over my eyes
did pass.

A mine of rubies… a hiding place, the pussy
is:
it, for you a place to rest, a silver pillow settee
is.
Nine months gone… quicksilver sperm left in it
is sprouting a moon that full of a face, lovely,
is!

As his wife was pregnant a judge was shouting,
crying:
he said aloud and out of spite… "What is really
happening?
I'm old… prick's head hasn't in ages been raided:
my whore is no Mary… who caused her to be
showing?"

If two days ago wind helmet of the narcissus was
raising…
then, a day back armour of the violet, down it was
throwing.
Today from water lily of the valley's sword, it took:
tomorrow… out of the rose's fire a shield it will be
making.

My heart is in your sad place, lonely too
it now is…
of your face rose is servant, whatever hue
it now is.
Water flowing nightly from my eyes turn
millstones, except your stony heart: true
it now is.

These eyes that were always working at seeing you
are now drowning in tears, do not let them this do!
And this heart that only had one occupation… you:
is now caught in your hair's lasso… so to it be true!

O you, whose face puts to shame the *huri* and
pari…*
and from which the sun, light has borrowed…
constantly;
from desire for your face and from it far away,
today I've thousands of tears on my face, you
see?

*Note: A huri is a beauty of Paradise in female form and a pari is a beauty in male form.

The cloud that blood keeps raining,
is grief for You:
poison that no antidote is having,
is grief for You.
What thousands full of grief never
in hearts or souls are experiencing,
is grief for You.

The cloud that raindrops is scattering
is grief for You…
like that which leaves one wondering,
is grief for You.
Although on fire me You are placing
is grief for You,
I'd be sad if what I was not having,
is grief for You!

Since before Time this heart was place of nesting
of Your Love…
for all of Eternity this soul of mine is the dwelling
of Your Love.
My soul and my heart I love because this heart has
Your brand on it and on my soul is sign, showing
of Your Love.

If, as it is said… that I had a thousand lives to
live,
before You each one I'd place… I would to You
give.
You asked: "Do you have heart for separation?"
Listen, if I'd one, I would have to try to be co-
operative.

If blood didn't continue to be flowing from these eyes
of mine
Your secret I could keep from this heart full of distress
of mine.
And if my breathing was not so cold and face so pale
I'd hide Your secret from heart… and soul, I stress…
of mine.

As my darling sat down beside the vein-opener,
vein-opener rose and of his hands was the tier…
as the sharp lance of his vein became the piercer,
see, from crystal's mine a ruby spring, a shooter!

I'm Mahsati and I'm most fair of those to be had,
I am famous for my beauty from Iraq to Meshad.
Preacher's boy, you're nothing but useless… bad:
if I get no bread, meat or prick, I get really mad!

That butcher boy, as is his usual way of doing
it,
threw me down, killed me, said, "I'm having
it!"
Then as an apology, he puts his head on my feet:
this, is to blow air under my skin, to be flaying
it.

*Note: This describes a method of skinning goats and sheep by butchers.
This poem is also attributed to the great Sufi poet
Sana'i who died in 1131 and would have met her at court when
she was 33 and would have been a big influence on her.
He also composed ribald ruba'is.
See my 'Ruba'iyat of Sana'i' New Humanity Books, 2012.

You shed such blood with those eyes, bloodthirsty,
of yours
and led astray many hearts with that hair, unruly,
of yours...
may God throw some mercy into your heart, so that
you may pay back those poor lovers, eventually...
of yours.

The world is on fire from what is in hearts
of ours...
the universe's confused due to hateful darts
of ours:
look at the goblet from which we drink water...
it is from kin, whose dust the earth imparts,
of ours.

Your cheeks are envied by rose and jasmine,
beloved
your flirting glance upsets men and women,
beloved.
On the way I found, like graceful running water,
water is running from my eyes again, again,
beloved.

Offering up prayers to idols in the temple
is uplifting;
praying, using a large winecup that is full,
is uplifting.
To say rosary upon hypocrisy's carpet never
is uplifting:
sacred thread worn in tavern is worshipful,
is uplifting.

There is a ditch that before that butcher is
lying...
every moment fresh blood into it keeps on
flowing;
how could blood like mine be of value when
to that one a thousand unjust murders, are
nothing?

Even at the point of an arrow, stopped…
I can't be,
and also in a gloomy cell kept, confined…
I can't be:
although tied by chain of your loving glance,
remaining inside of this house, chained…
I can't be!

Ah no… around your roses thorns have been
growing;
like a crow has come and in its beak a tulip is
taking.
Your chin bright as quicksilver… is tarnished,
and the vermilion of your ruby lips all lustre is
losing.

O breeze, I would give my life for a message
delivered,
if you pass where that one born of a *huri* has
resided…
say, that upon the way, throwing her precious
life away out of love for you… Mahsati you
discovered.

How could I ever tell what my love for you,
did to me:
what your heart full of deceit, hypocrisy too,
did to me?
The night, it should be as long as your long hair,
so I can tell to you what separation from you
did to me.

O king… praise and eulogy is all I can be offering
to you:
prayers from a humble woman are enough to bring
to you.
I am no cow and horns are not meant for me to have;
were I one, two horns would be what I'd be giving
to you.*

Note: The custom of drinking wine from horns.

The very core, the substance of my life… has passed away:
meaning… beloved's curls from these hands slipped away.
I dyed my hands with *henna* for sake of my beloved:
but, as I went to sleep my sweetheart, quietly… fled away.

Time, it has decided this… that for as long as it may,
it won't let my heart's desire happen, even for a day.
Heaven determined… around Earth it will revolve,
to make me pass through misfortune with no delay.

Who could the thief be? When the house he's entering,

from fear through the windows the house is escaping...

the house is fleeing and the thief for goods is searching,

after the house has gone all those goods he's seizing!*

*Note: This is one of her famous 'riddle ruba'is'. The answer is the thief is a fishing net and the house is the water.

O son of the preacher of Ganjeh, take this advice of mine,*

sit on the throne of pleasure and hold tight the cup of wine:

God is indifferent to devotion, and to transgression;

so, however it is in this world, to your heart's desire resign.

*Note: This poem is written to the son of a preacher, the poet Taju'd-din Amir Ahmad... whom she either married or became the mistress of... see her life etc., introduction.

I discovered that one, lying drunk… upon the way:
I fell at that one's feet; that hand in mine I did lay.
That one does not remember any bit of this…
that is, I don't remember but that one does, today.

I am a new blooming rose that no thorn is having,
or a warbling nightingale that its grief is sharing,
or falcon with seat on hands of monarchs,
that has fallen into Your trap: well, it be keeping.

Book in one hand, holding winecup in other

are we;

now to faith and now to heresy, as a turner,

are we:

both frail and fickle, heaven's canopy under,

are we;

absolute heathens, perfect Muslims, neither

are we.

That your promise was quite fuzzy,

I knew:

that it would be broken… trust me,

I knew!

This wrong, my friend, that so unjustly

you lately did to me, O so early…

I knew!

To be sucking your ruby lips, forever,

I am longing,

to with you take wine in sips, forever,

I am longing.

Whether intoxicated, mad or sober… to

hear harp from your fingertips forever

I am longing.

You are a butcher to me, while in your love, burning

am I;

that your knife may reach these very bones… trying

am I.

Your practice is to sell whatever you have butchered…

heaven's sake, if me you kill, don't sell me: begging,

am I!

Like some feeble bird, without feathers and wing

I am,

caught in a trap, no one knowing my suffering…

I am:

an illness has been attacking this heart of mine…

and so, today, terribly afflicted, crying, wailing

I am.

Each night from loving you another torture, suffering
am I;
each night, instead of sleep, with eyes, tears flowing,
am I.
When your narcissus eyes snatched my sleep away…
than what is wilder than your wild curls… dreaming,
am I.

O Beloved, I'll not stoop low for you…
even not for one, superior to you, too!
I'll not even at Jamshid look, it's true:*
in water I'll lie, never get wet through.

*Note: Jamshid is a king of ancient Iran.

It's true… drunkards, winehouse frequenters
we are,
neither devotees, nor any hermits, nor seers,
we are.
Judge drinks no wine, fears it: theft in tavern
beats orphan-robbing… not making smears,
we are.

In the snare of love there's none as grief-stricken
as me:
due to your torture there is none as heart-broken
as me.
There are many who are falling in love with you:
in faithfulness, there is none as true, I say again,
as me.

More fresh than Merv's tulip is that son, of the
muezzin...*
put to shame the pheasant's blood has that one's
complexion:
when fame of that one's graceful stature spread...
then cypress stood, as though in prayer... in the
garden.

*Note: One who calls the people to prayer.

It is love that makes the wild lion tame...
and it is from the ocean that comes again
a wonder: now like soul-refreshing friend
it acts, now like blood-thirsty foe, insane!

Like a horse... you gallop sprightly in the field of joy,
with subtle ingenuity you do wonders, not being coy;
with queen, king, pawns, clergy, castles, knights...
you play excellently and elegantly, skilfully, my boy.

Careful... or you may come into a winehouse most profane,
unless you act like a *rend*... there, nothing you will attain.
Here is path of *rends* not caring if they're criticized:
they're unafraid: unless you risk your life, you can't gain.

Wine cup one of our hands holds, a *Koran* the other...
we're sometimes awake or we're in a drunken stupor!
Who are we really in this world that is so frail?
We're not a Zoroastrian, not a real Muslim either.

Wind through the hand for what exists is all remaining…
because everything is immutable and has an ending.
Remember, that all that exists is not really existing…
and what isn't existing, it's as though it's something.

When in need don't wait for help from another…
O heart, a withered reed they'd never offer.
Stinginess creates beasts, thrift is the sustainer…
so if you become poor, don't be a big spender.

Nothing stops us: moment's fate, arrows at us…
not even wild longing, our hearts to hold, to truss.
My soft braids were steel chains in your heart:
but could a chain hold me if I wish to roam, thus?

There's a world for those who mines of jewels desire…
poets desire a different world, their throne is higher.
Bird eating love's magic grain is on a plane, finer…
nests beyond both worlds; of riches, fame, a scorner.

All columns in your house, and all bricks seen,
are from heads of kings, fingers of some queen.
And each bit of earth where your cattle graze,
from hair hiding cheek of fair beloved has been.

From when we climbed pinnacle, love minaret,
we've known no words but love's... passionate.
None should cross love's threshold, our home:
its hearth is ice cold, love's fiery grace too late!

This is my heart, it is what love that is true,
means...
love that brings me pain like others... it, too
means.
This poor heart produces each sigh and bitter cry:
this, is my heart... this is what love of you,
means.

I happened to see a man on the road, yesterday,
swinging the rod he had as he went on his way.
Some slave of a wife of his, he beat furiously...
those passing watched without sign of dismay.

Winehouse is museum of brave, hall of notoriety...
none here who are low or mean may the inside see.
All who set foot inside here must pay due respect:
in here, none by deceit one may find... believe me.

If Egypt, China, Byzantium all belong to
you,
then it follows that all the world you own
too.
Your life make happy, for in the end your plot
is a sheet and hole into where you they
threw.

When tying the knot a man to a woman is tied...
in God's eye this is good, a law... true and tried.
The knot of marriage, is tying me to my *ruba'i*...
is there a faith that would make me so inspired?

As if in a daze, lying by canal in a field you're
dreaming...
O moon-faced angel, willow-thin, over stream
bending.
Down hill I come bathed in sunlight direct to you:
O lovely one, do not think for water I came...
hurrying!

From your hair, such a pleasant fragrance
comes...
morning breeze takes it up, to it dispense,
comes.
If an ascetic sees your charms as we embrace...
can he bear dryness, and not to his sense
comes?

The rose said, "Before I had time to open these
eyes,
before joy's berry I'd plucked from life's earthly
paradise...
I was plucked by hands to take my scent's essence:
may hands also be cut from life... cut down to
size."

On green grass the rose grows in quiet ecstasy,
nightingale sings out song, a fervent rhapsody!
Each in bliss, forgetting how the spell began…
rose in its brief life, nightingale in grief, lonely.

O my love, come, press your tender lips to mine;
bring me back to life, so from your love like wine
I can… blind drunk, be clay within your hands,
and to know world's woe or not I won't incline.

Though you, crowned head, may be lord of all,
one day you may cry from poverty… take a fall.
Let folk move heart, be near them, love them…
fear the day you will need help, them you'll call!

Nothing can bind us: moment's pull, arrows accuracy,
no mad nostalgia that seizes our heart with a frenzy!
Though my braids turned into steel to anchor in your
heart… could chain keep me at home if I wish to flee?

Your curls are long… like all my sorrows
are,
you treat servants well but still my woes
are!
My eyes, your beautiful eyes are not loving…
no balm from me they needing, it shows
are!

When from these eyes, tears… rose-coloured
fall,
afterwards thousands more, colour of blood…
fall!
This heart has been burnt in the fire of your love
and though it's burnt, blood does still indeed
fall!

Rosebud-like arrows the flower was growing
to with your beauty, beloved, be competing!
When from far off your face's sun took blade,
it… arrows shields destroyed by penetrating!

Arrow from ready bow of that dark Turk fired
away,
its target in heart of unworthy lovers will hit,
anyway.
That one is the kind of Turk who is alert enough
to two eggs in the dark night be juggling… his
foray!

All in this city, men and women, see your
face,
and from fire and grief and you… danger
face!
All clothing in a year your father sells is less
than what daily they tear off, due to your
face!

O Ganjeh's chief preacher, my advice be accepting…
sit upon joy's seat and a brimming cup be holding!
God doesn't have a need for guilt and bowing:
with wine and a pretty one heart your be enlivening!

Between the house of faith and faithlessness,
is a breath;
between the stages of doubt and positiveness
is a breath.
Be thankful for the most precious breath of all…
because the very fruit of our life and no less,
is a breath

The winds to roses to the drunkards scatter,
came...
I to wine on that tongue as the joyful pourer
came!
That one to kill the squirrel than my navel lower,
came...
to bring disgrace to rose that one with amber
came!

Tell me, tell me, why don't you ever listen,
learn?
Your eyes thirst for blood, nothing is seen:
learn!
Your eyebrows you touch-up, O you mad killer!
To be human, you know... have you been?
Learn!

Beautiful one, you said: "My grapes are heavenly:
in this nest you'll find a thousand gems... to see."
Are these words you utter true, or are they false...
who has courage to speak out about this, only me?

The flowers were all amazed because the rose
was embarrassed...
this mouth of mine when I tasted it, I suppose
was embarrassed!
Weight it up if there is any obscenity in your heart...
if you're rude it's a shame one with such a pose
was embarrassed!

To my enemies you've always talked about me;
you come to caress, but my face you turn sourly.
Behind all these scenes games are being played:
enough, with your tenderness you've scared me!

"For one bushel," I said, "my lips are a
guest!"
"For a bushel," the reply... "My soul's
quest!"
My heart pounded so much it struck my side,
that I did call: "Ah boy, where is this
priest?"

In chains I need to keep you and you keep
me...
so at evening we aren't seeking another to
see!
I talked of my pain before I became enchanted:
don't laugh at me for being drunk, as you'll
be!

At evening, that one again caught me intoxicated...
that one blinked on seeing it then to run off started.
I shouted: "It's night and it's too late can't you see;
please, in this state they'll suddenly see us parted!"

Nightingale, was drunk again yesterday morning...
that one did arrive for the good news to be having.
To those breezes that one said, "O for God's sake,
in village what's wrong with rose one's touching?"

That one opened mouth to hear a tired question
from me...
"How many servants have you kissed? It's one,
from me?"
Your heart and eyes look happy with your promise;
you took to the road, away from the situation,
from me!

See how by your heart truly humiliated
you are...
see what doing to one who oppressed...
you are?
Do you understand the heart, book of love?
One day waking from having dreamed
you are!

Look at my body, my heart inside is
broken!
Look at my soul... a storm of fire has
fallen!
Look in my eyes, rose from love of your face
has tears that're always flowing into
ocean!

How much blood did you by one eye shed,
Zulfun, tell me... how many hearts ruined?
May great God grant justice to your heart:
possibly, of love affairs you've been cured?

Month of beauty won't other than itself be:
that one never wakes even through sorcery!
From moment you draw the line around it,
not a drop of blood escaping will be, really!

They take a line out of the sweating violet,
from the flower...
to moon drawing line, what does heart get
from the flower?
It was always late at night near to the dawn.
from a night that gave birth, don't forget,
from the flower!

Don't shed tears, to this work you're a stranger;
O let me grieve, or rejoice, rejoice, or... whatever!
This lover can no longer cry, tears be shedding:
O you poor thing leave it to me; be free, forever!

Enough is enough patience... O rose, don't break!
Enough of oppression, the promise don't forsake!
Even if it doesn't matter, answer is write a letter!
Don't burn me in the fire... just the answer take!

I caught up again with that one in the evening...
from date-lips a hundred kisses I was receiving!
Lover wanted to tell me of love with each kiss...
as that mouth began to swear it I was stopping!

I said: "Don't hurt me, don't get so hot...
you!
We'll see God, you be true, come quickly
too."
In a fever you... "Asma talks more than you
do:
I burn for that one more, don't turn away,
you!"

And so, this is how it turned out to be,
my heart...
I fear my soul will be destroyed totally
my heart!
And you, you haven't lost one small thing:
in my language I apologize, stupidly,
my heart!

That fate, that tragedy my heart suffered...
with much longing my heart always ached!
With light, heart lit a candle in my house...
in my heart a thousand jewels I discovered!

Sweetheart, look at that purple, so pleasing...
sulphur, fire in desert caught, colour creating!
That one who is grieving is all bent over now,
yet... the scent's as beautiful as in the spring!

> One eye is longing for the ways to be a
> seer:
> don't be blind to crying with difficulty,
> ever!
> It was a sick heart that loved you, only you...
> you're womb's captive but my respect's
> there!

No matter how much a heart from sorrow
bleeds,
no matter how many lives one gives up one
needs;
have mercy upon me… it doesn't rain from heaven,
forgive; to blush, heart in dirt does no such
deeds!

No human being could be so intelligent, clever…
lovable Mehreen, I'm amazed by your demeanour.
I'm happy now my friend, but from start of night
that I may suddenly die was the cause of my fear.

You with words, freed me from sorrow that day,
you did;
you made heart joyful with a promise yesterday,
you did!
If, what you said that day, was to be coming out…
you might remember the promise you gave: say
you did!

My heart's now closed to you, wrong was done by
me...
there was really no love, heart hurts, so don't try
me!
I went into mourning, but you went into rejoicing...
God keep you alone, I'm going... gone: but, why
me?

I don't talk about love, in the heart appearing
let it be...
on the contrary, in my eyes, not just anything
let it be.
Let love not be in my heart and not in my eyes...
never, in this country or sea, any hell rising
let it be!

Every night your deep sorrow, O so painful
I saw...
my eyes wet with sadness and of desire full,
I saw!
Narcissus deceived eye, dream disappeared...
never such a sweet dream in my life to recall
I saw.

Everyone, through love burning, burning away
was...
in the evening lying everywhere a bloody spray
was!
The world knows in the world is the tent of love...
standing far from heaven that one the next day
was.

Where is night from... what is love's
way?
That one knows that one's troubles
today!
If people reveal a secret that will destroy it
if one hides it, grief will kill straight
away!

With love to my burning heart you'd set fire,
over and over you saw the water get higher!
Did you see my hair, you approved my luck?
Toss those black curls onto the ground, liar!

How sorrowful I was, look at your eunuch:
friends cried at me like foes... I was unique!
Out of love for you I moaned all the time...
all night the candle burned my heart's tunic.

What can satisfy you, what can I in return do
easily?
If you kill me, what religion says do it, you...
easily?
What a pleasure it is to remember any stranger...
to like anything or anyone, doesn't come too
easily!

Tell me, what happened to all those promises?
You go on circulating, promising another says.
Your words, were honeyed, 'Why not, us sin?'
They, have become poison, no one says, 'Yes!'

I open heart, I'm sorry, but talk is all I can
do:
I don't have strength from grief... for you,
too!
Even if it should cross mind to write a letter,
in my heart I don't have strength, power
to.

That one was taking my heart by oppression
and if that one returns I will never away run!
Let that one stand desperately on Last Day:
at least I won't go down with no explanation!

It's so obvious that I've done so much
crying,
so much that I was frightened to be
thinking.
Come, if you see me more tender that water,
it was such tenderness causing my
moaning.

That cloud of sorrow brings grief and desires;

and, that sorrow may end in a hundred years.

Neylim is the oppressor, creator of this fate;

the agony has hit me with such cruelty, fears!

Even if the water behind that one doesn't flow

I will never abandon humanity to you, so... go!

You have asked me what I did to you; tell me...

what you did to me that outside doesn't show?

    Look at the earth, the earth, the water too,
            O sweetheart...
    look at the sky and the sun shining through,
            O sweetheart!
If I see you I'll die, out of breath; from jealousy
I'll let go this form if another dreams of you,
            O sweetheart!

It's a cloud of grief dropping blood from the eyes
and pain's a poison that can't be cured I surmise.
It's an agony that breaks the heart each moment:
grief never leaves heart or soul where health lies.

From my face tears were flowing from sorrow...
pain:
in that one doing the oppression does not grow,
pain!
If I burn I'll be in the fire from that pain from you:
I burn from grief and if you go, eyes will know
pain!

If you're not side by side me in this sorrow, who
will...
my eyes cry blood, your heart's full of blood, you
will?
You are now longing for a love that is a new love?
O heart, what can I say, this victim of love too
will!

You are always tricking me and my hands tying...
Zulfun, you will end up pagan idols worshipping.
When you say farewell to your narcissus at dawn,
catch hold of that one, to keep that one drinking!

The moon shone in the sky breaking out its face...
back of cypress, the cypress broke, it's a disgrace!
With the blood out of my heart I took this my life:
to you I went to sacrifice it, I burnt without trace!

That one doesn't know why my heart so eloquent
has become...
what draws my heart, white my hair, it's evident
has become!
O no! O no! Why... are you still sleeping at night?
Now, you can see how at night sleep an event...
has become?

"If your poor face is not hairy, then it's all bloody!"
"But, how are you knowing that my dear, tell me."
"Your face may smell of musk but that is useless!"
"Even if it is useless, there's a lot of blood to see?"

    I am so fortunate to be one separated,
        today
    tomorrow store of grief in my heart will
        stay.
    Enough blood, O my eyes, stop crying blood:
    heart, burn in the fire, was what you did
        say!

Your face, it is pink like freshly picked roses,
and you are so charming like the tall cypress.
The nightingale asks in a voice full of sorrow:
"Is another in this world who that smile sees?

In a room with love your soul's fine, but less
is less...
on your face are hardly any tears, my guess...
is less!
It is pleasant like a comb to go through your hair,
but if one looks at hair's curls, there, I stress,
is less!

If that one, self sees, that one's humiliated...
for light of the sun by the heavens is shared!
Our faces are always longing to see flowers:
if we leave, our faces by tears... will be filled!

My breath in my chest, don't without You...
let it be:
let any heart without You be destroyed, too:
let it be!
If in my heart I had a little joy, not only grief...
then, all of whole body imprisoned for You.
let it be!

If there was no bloodshed I'd look hard again:

me!

Your secret, in this heart I would hide… then:

me!

If not, this sallow face would drop tears from eyes

for every secret was cherished by one of them:

me!

If, a hundred thousand souls I was having,

I'd openly, every one of them be sacrificing!

If in your heart you've patience to say this…

if I'd a heart, none of it, would be escaping?

First, before me, heart I was showing

You,

I was quiet before I gave love my heart

too.

Praise be to God, my heart's Your servant;

it is like my guts I spilled out; that, is

true!

Night's come, world's gone into darkness,
one was so fortunate to be awake, no less!
To the moon, the sun said: "I am so tired!"
Grief's wheel mind's circle broke, no mess!

Why in dark night do you grieve, tell
me?
You are strong, not as thin as this
body!
If all your lovers you cannot appreciate...
you aren't in love, a lover don't try to
be!

The trees were drinking the autumn
dew...
in a dream that one's drunk a year or
two!
In the gardens the flowers, all tulips open:
meadow is like an oasis in a desert,
anew!

Narrow-hearted grief the field has chosen...
the roses are amazed to see face of that one.
That heart of stone these tears don't soften:
tell, what heart of stone, in what dungeon?

No matter how much we don't want, grieving
there is...
many types, or flavours of love to be having...
there is!
The time of separation's here, talk in one tongue:
in a moment how many a world you be seeing
there is!

Whenever the tears from out of these eyes
are spilling,
moon's light pours down on me... like seas
are spilling!
On the day I left you, I was shedding blood...
if more leaves my body, all down to knees
are spilling!

Longing is still in my sad heart, this one
says...
my grief wanders with me, I this woman
says.
Can I sacrifice my heart for love of my life?
It's a dream in my mind, this one again
says.

Your life for love, you have to be sacrificing...
do you:
don't rejoice, you know life it is destroying...
do you?
You cannot even see a speck of what it all means:
give pain to Afghans, you want to be going,
do you?

See beautiful Shahla, that God-mad woman;
from Afghanistan, comes that drunken one...
if for a moment that one makes the hair dance,
a hundred fights break out as hearts dance on!

I said: "My life is useless, futile, have mercy!"
Answer: "The world was ruined by jealousy!"
I asked this: "If I die will you give me a kiss?"
Answer was: "Tell me when did you ask me?"

I will sacrifice each river flowing behind me,
my God...
I am a fiery character and on my way to see
my God!
All lands of Yours to be known I'm enslaved by:
I love the winds that blow scents magically,
my God.

From Your grace sorrow turns into happiness,
one can look back upon such a heavenly caress!
If when breeze blows it reaches a nearby land...
suddenly Water of Life from fire we can access!

If that one oppresses me, the baker's charming;
not with being angry but with all that flirting.
I was like the dough left in the hand of sorrow:
this is my fear, that the fire's only half blazing!

On your pistachio there is laughter, you flirt!
Your face, is like this day… beautiful, bright!
I see it burns as you are grinding the grater…
nothing wrong there, you're unique at night!

We've witnessed how cruel oppression can be;
like sorrow we were falling because of enemy.
Play chess straight on the throne of fidelity…
but one day it might be dull… O I'm so sorry!

Dartar's bow keeps raising those particular
arrows...
shoots in chest of lover those popular poplar
arrows!
Look closely and you can see how agile that one is;
wake at night due to blows of those regular
arrows!

Forgetful one plundering throne of spring
did...
madly intoxicated, me brought to moaning
did!
O my apple-cheek, I keep longing for the peach...
like quince I turned yellow as one bleeding
did!

The shoemaker gives the shoe every adornment:
from time to time Lali touches it in wonderment.
Shoe, will finally be adorned with honey kisses...
sun in the heavens is crowned... a terrible event?

Your letter, it shot me down just yesterday...
then, sweat-spiking winds all blew me away!
Without you, I am a lily in the water today...
sweetheart we're finished tomorrow, anyway!

In Nishapour fire broke out among the roses;
in Merv yesterday on water-lilies... showers.
In Herat, the wind will today blow for hours;
it is possible, in Balkh tomorrow, ambergris!

That day, tulips drew from the fire a
dagger;
yesterday the lily was thrown into the
water!
O wind, today full of straw is your
armour...
on the helmet tomorrow put bud of a
flower!

Muezzin boy who looks like a tulip sweating,

on seeing, face goes red, shame is it covering.

In world when boy's words fell from the sky,

in admiration cypress bowed head, gasping!*

*Note: From minaret of the mosque the muezzin calls the faithful to prayer.

There are twists and turns from the Chinese
and China...
where does the line meet between all these...
and China?
From possession of the Chinese the *Huri* escaped:
the world gave you its word, word is 'please':
and, China?*

*Note: A huri is a beautiful maiden of Paradise.

You've no longer strength to be half-hearted…

no:

I've no longer the fire an heart that's heated…

no!

I can see no more trace of fires once in my heart:

sweetheart, has no more beauty manifested…

no!

When you saw that one you hoped for a share

O thread…

like a wind towards Lali you went wherever,

O thread!

Why is it that life is so rough upon the needle?

You're just a pinch in that water of life, her,

O thread!

Your face is a candle, O beauty, heart's butterfly:

we are the mad who into love fall from a cruel lie!

One day make a decree the help will give us love:

that help is one with a white face… lips that fly!

"You must be happy, dear, so eloquent, so playful!
Lovers should moan a thousand times, be rueful!"
You answer... "I have your heart, I've taken it!"
I replied: "You take it, but you return it... in full!"

Even if you build a single nest out of stone,
O winebringer...
death that comes can be foolish for anyone,
O winebringer!
My dear, earth you should read is just dry land:
the wind is its breath: start with just one,
O winebringer!

Though you be on the road like dust trampled,
yes...
and even if like the winds you've finally fled,
yes...
now listen to me, even if that one saves your life
even if on fire, don't take water from dead...
yes?

I'd a strange conversation with that one that day:
I asked this, "Are you satisfied, with me... say!"
Reply: "Of course, open mouth... say one word!"
I said, "What to say?" Reply... "My lucky day!"

That sugarcane is never at mouth narrow only:
that flower sweats like a rose, smiling sweetly.
From your love this heart's in a hundred pieces:
what's the remedy for eyelashes defeating me?

If you're all salty, it's because you're a fool...
you!
You're like a fresh flower... fresh kind of tool,
you!
I learnt milk you sucked from some tender breast:
if you're a prophet you're more like a ghoul...
you!

Last night there was a wind going on and on;
my eyes that beautiful road then turned upon.
Night crept away; at dawn I felt blindfolded:
"Don't!" I said, "God, my trouble has begun!"

O Turk, O God, into those arms take me!
To some other place be taking me, quickly!
In any case all my work is now in disarray:
the two sad eyes of mine hurry up and see!

The black wind blew the burnt ones clothes...
burnt were half the descendants of a species!
I woke, stood and I went to snuff the candle:
I saw all candles are gone, where went these?

Yesterday the nightingale was in the dust
again
and all hearts in the world were set on fire,
then.
O friend, today some water was thrown at you;
my dove, the morning wind no sand sent
again.

Out of love, sifting the sand I went nowhere...
out of grief I didn't talk to anyone, didn't care!
Gold in my hand I searched for you each day...
you sifted the soil but for gold, your full share!

I am Mahsati, I'm not happy and I don't care
about in Iraq and Khorasan, those dead there!
O Puri-Khatibi-Ganjeh... O God, come here...
in the fire don't let me be burnt as it isn't fair!

O rose... if as a servant we your face remember,
and if with Zulfun we make your heart happier,
we then with you have played chess once again
but we shouldn't overdo it by being an offender.

O my soul, of my heart the medicine is prayer...
in garden where is rose, to your face remember?
By your beauty the Chinese were embarrassed:
look at such a beauty, see the world as lovelier!

One day two tailors had come into the
square,
the king to complain had suddenly gone
there.
Arranda, he then ordered those master tailors:
"You can take needle from king, but not
here!"

I saw that beautiful young man in Sarrajan:
it's not necessary to be one's soul if one can!
Such a one, will eventually mourn another...
thousand times in soul love will grow again!

Zulfun is now thirty and perhaps
intoxicated;
being thirty that one's asleep, or…
inebriated.
That one's neck looks like ivory, or all silvery:
even if one buys thirty bushels it's
celebrated!

Every time I smile it's always in one direction:
take hair from your face or it, blood will fall on.
If out of love that fire is burning like a candle…
a woman burns on one side on the other a man!

I saw the beautiful boy on the chimney yesterday:
I told to that one to breathe in the beauty today…
That one, showed no mercy to this heart, no pity:
smoke rose from the chimney, it swept me away!

A good habit to go and be drinking,
this is:
if a friend, fidelity to us swearing...
this is!
That face of the road known as the world,
how to look at it, as an imagining...
this is?

Blood of my soul is upon me like a scorpion;
my faith from me by love's arrow was taken.
Line crossed as it were, by order of the King:
in other words trust is left to God, the One!

At times my eyes are a benefit, at times
hurting;
low or high, far or near... or I forget to be
looking.
The strange thing is that one's a friend and foe...
openly saying: "For better or worse, I am
being!"

That one's face amazes both men and women:
my heart is troubled and my spirit is in pain...
many garments, that one sells over the years:
my friend, in a day to fall in love, once again?

The wind blew over the tulips and roses that day,
the deserts have passed away, earth passed away!
Brother, if life you drink do it and don't be tricked:
if tomorrow, you burn in the fires, ashes will stay!

That one kills with a knife but halfway through
in those lips that one places it, it is terrible too!
And if that one's stabbing another one to death,
that soul that was killed, that killer kills, anew!

The butcher boy was standing in the shop
again,
from right to the left customers waited, in
vain?
That one said to them as a hand pulled at meat:
"Well done me, not the Buddha, *my* arm
again!"

When in love this world is a paradise for me...
only grief I have is when your face I don't see.
Why, did you lay me down upon this carpet...
or, is it only habit of yours, is it... customary?

The blacksmith's boy came with a horseshoe;
I was amazed when the horse bent for a shoe.
In this world, who has seen a sight like this?
Strike a crescent moon upon that horseshoe!

Gone were all bloody burns, that one rejoiced:
the bleeding was clamped tightly, no more red!
It was as though coral sweated out of crystal:
the scalpel struck a vein and it stung, instead.

The beautiful boys from Chigil were coming:
O Lord, how much dust, are they kneading?
Bodies are silver, lips of honey, words sugar:
Lord, how were such happy souls happening?

It's a heart's cold winter, rose-face, just prose:
all one's enemies are loved, for us hate grows.
It seems luck's tossed us a long unlucky fate;
otherwise, you wouldn't have given us woes!

In spring don't choose another place on water
and with that lilac-faced one don't get closer.
Brush hair halfway through, smell ambergris,
and other than rosy wine do not be a drinker!

    I'm swearing to you, upon Jesus, my
                             dear,
    if you come here to us turn away from
                             fear.
    Wipe away tears from my eyes, each
                             tear,
    your dripping lips touch mine, am I
                             clear?

If you rub in the ambergris... you, are spoiled:
how can the world not be in chaos embroiled?
If you're roaming about on the seven plagues
why don't you come here to me, very scared?

To be counting what has been ruined
don't come...
to take hand of a bridesmaid offered,
don't come!
Everyone who comes and goes is here, now...
and if you have not away yet passed,
don't come!

If, you ride a happy horse you'll the field open:
be admiring the magic of nature's population.
Horse, elephant, ball, field, or any pedestrian:
master, if you play with agility... easy to win!

Laugh and look at the red roses in the meadow,
then turn a stormy winter into spring on show!
You knew that I'd never give up for I'm a rose:
so, now go and send off the violet, tell it to go!

In my heart, there is, O... you boy, so cunning,
a bird of sorrow, that was a long time leaving.
In the twist in my heart there is such a curling
knowing only snakes from snakes are coming!

The abode of my soul in the ship has long been;
I've been friends with you forever, it does seem!
Love from my soul and heart goes to you, lover:
in both a mountain and communication is pain!

My dear, one who blood's shedding, is blessed:
that one's a cruel tyrant if that one's deceived!
You came then took revenge on this poor lover:
look in my eyes, see how much blood you shed!

I'd loved you but saw how much I hated
you:
Ah, my friend, it is like running water...
true?
Either I have sinned, caught up in such anger,
or there's another tomorrow: it's hidden
too!

Tell me: this loneliness and burning in here,
there is?
Such a heart as mine, smashed by whoever...
there is?
In this game of love there are many new players:
my one and only promise I was given forever;
there... is?

Friend, you're rememberer of my words, always;
your thoughts are with me through nights, days.
Don't be criticizing my work it brings nothing...
fires in heart are from God, this moaning stays.

I have gone, but heart of mine will be staying
here...
there will be sympathy for pain it's suffering
here!
My body has gone too, just like it always goes...
but of my heart Your love care will be taking
here!

I still go on hiding from this, my weakness,
it's a secret:
from my pen, no matter what you're saying:
it's a secret!
My body's melting and I'm sighing once or twice:
so now from you in the bathroom I'm hiding:
it's a secret!

Mouth, eyes, tulip-faced, cheerful, handsome too:
apple cheeks, almond eyes, pistachio mouth, you!
How small that mouth of yours is and those eyes:
impossible to cry over them, or laugh... as you do!

We love neither the rug nor the prostration,
it is all a waste of time, like being in a ruin!
If one doesn't drink wine it's a body's fault:
good luck in a world of orphans, to that one.

I have no wings, I'm a poor bird, I'm helpless:
I fell into Your net, being of You unconscious.
This soul of mine is so weary of this life I live:
everywhere my work was greeted by distress!

> You, are like some dove, O so charming...
> you the peacock cry with joy are making!
> From my chest heart's pigeons are flying:
> through door you are a peacock entering!

Have mercy, please go to the bathroom, early:
sleep well tonight so we may rest peacefully.
I'll be up early, and then go off to the village:
with my heart I say, "I'll get water... plenty!"

From the fire in my heart to the time of fire...
world will be too old as my fire grows higher.
The lands of my brothers have passed away...
we now get drunk, if we drink a jug of water!

   O wheel of fortune, this old world ruining
                    you did...
   with oppression the kingdom's plundering
                    you did!
O earth, if your breast's torn and you're angry,
    see how swallowing gems then bleeding
                    you did!

In all ways I have never seen any loyalty

from you...

yes, it's a complaint, but nothing will be

from you.

My friend, to you this world is as an enemy seen:

go, leave why should I expect any story,

from you?

What sin have I done for you to show me hatred

and why did you suffer so much that oppressed?

That is what happened and after that just pity:

enough blood is shed, no guilt in heart, wasted!

My heart is just a flower, face a rose...

rejoice!

Wherever you are, come, bring joy to my

voice!

The only thing that's a pair are your eyebrows:

a pair, one with that neck, a shadow so

choice!

I came home and was there anything here?

No!

Was something heart desires... even near?

No!

You say that here everything is plentiful... yes?

There is nothing here, no blessing is there:

no!

If you are old who will bring us together...

like branches;

in a house full of sorrows who'll us gather

like branches?

O sheikh, my chain is like a jewel, look at it!

Us in this chain, who'll take the weather,

like branches?

Tenderly, through the night I slept; they all
are gone:
days I was pierced by grief, I cannot recall...
are gone!
You were my soul and my heart and conspirator...
but now all those old times, large and small
are gone!

I swear by the sun in the sky, by God's face...
let it be!
I swear by the day my hair was my disgrace...
let it be!
O my soul, my heart, I will water you with tears...
by God, that one is yours, any time or place:
let it be!

O rose, be in my heart and everywhere,
together,
for this world is ruby wine made for the
drinker.
Friend, whatever night you may stay with me...
in the daytime I want us both to be gone
forever.

O wind, may your howling tongue be sacrificed:
you're only halfway there, you should have fled!
Quickly tell Mahsati what on the way you saw:
"That one, who life for you sacrificed, is dead!"

To make a half-hat, feels a sweet thing to do...
who see it say a thousand words or two, to you!
Each day one is wearing the dazzling satin hat,
and those threads on it, are silver and gold too!

O you king, it is enough for you from me...
it's enough...
a prayer from a helpless woman, obviously
it's enough!
This one is not a bull so why do you need horns?
it'd be enough if I were, but I'm not... see?
It's enough!

Drawing bow, showing strength of shoulder,
you...
see how the arrow is kissing mouth of holder:
you!
It's as if you had torn that shaft from my words...
no matter what you want not enough to hear
you.

In your heart is disbelief; what is faith, prayer?
Dear, in the past is this poison, what's a cure?
You introduced yourself everywhere as a hermit:
if it is not true, the blood becomes a high fever!

The tears of sorrow are always flowing freely;
what will you do, you who cut off love for me?
With respect I say, that this age is a caravan:
it comes from heart's Ka'ba to wait patiently!

If that one worships idols, in them I'll
believe:
if given wine it's good to intoxication
receive.
I am not here to be in love with anyone, O no:
but if I should receive love... it will me
relieve!

My heart longs for the chance to love, suddenly:
but, let's talk about grief that breaks heart of me.
I do not know about all those naughty bastards...
but they rain from sky, from ground grow wildly.

If you are intending to be travelling...

O Sarvan;

don't reject you will not be passing...

O Sarvan!

Although the camel carries a load, you

my load of grief are still carrying...

O Sarvan!

Upon Lali to be kissing and sucking

I dream...

to with that one the wine be drinking

I dream!

If I'm intoxicated, dead drunk, or awake...

to be upon that one's hook jumping...

I dream.

Wait, come... what a beautiful hideaway

I have...

I decorated it all; to you, life gave away

I have!

Come quickly, for I have *kebabs* with wine...

giving with heart and soul so you'll stay

I have!

APPENDIXES...

MAHSATI GANJAVI IN THE STUDIES OF BRITISH ORIENTALISTS

The article deals with the research of British orientalists about Mahsati Ganjavi. It is noted that Mahsati Ganjavi is a great Azerbaijani poetess of the XII century. She wrote her works mainly in Persian, was known among creative people as the author of rubai. The purpose of the article is to bring together all the studies about Mahsati Ganjavi, carried out by British orientalists from the early XX century to the present, and to provide the main details mentioned in these researches. The article uses methods of analysis of manuscript data, as well as a method of comparison. The novelty of the article is to study all the researches about Mahsati Ganjavi made in the UK, and to provide important information about the manuscript of the novel "Mahsati and Amir Ahmad", which is stored in the British Library, as well as a ceramic bowl decorated with Mahsati Ganjavi's rubai in the Victoria and Albert Museum in London. Results. In 2013, UNESCO decided to celebrate the 900th anniversary of Mahsati Ganjavi in the world. Mahsati Ganjavi's bold poetry has been translated into many languages, including English, and is studied by British orientalists. Professor Edward Brown wrote about Mahsati Ganja in his book "A Literary History of Persia". In turn, Meredith Owens in 1969 published an article on the manuscript of the novel "Mahseti and Amir Ahmad", which is in the British Library. Another recent study by Marley Hammond provides information on Mahsati Ganjavi, as well as a ceramic bowl decorated with the Mahsati

Ganjavi rubai, which is housed in the Victoria and Albert Museum in London. Mahsati Ganjavi's biography and some of her rubai were translated in the book Borrowed Ware, written by orientalist Dick Davis. In 2013, the BBC aired a program about Mahsati Ganjavi, presented by Nargez Farzad. Conclusions. Thus, all these studies are very important for the recognition of Mahsati Ganjavi in the world and consideration of her life and work. The translation of such bold poetry into English plays an important role in the recognition and study of Azerbaijani classical literature not only in Great Britain but also in the world. Key words: Mahsati Ganjavi, Azerbaijani literature, rubai, language of poetry, free-thinking, feminist ideas, intimate poetry. Introduction. Mahsati Ganjavi is the most prominent poetess of the 12th century Azerbaijani literature. She was born in Ganja, the second largest city of the Republic of Azerbaijan. Mahsati is famous for her Rubaiyat. Rubaiyat is the plural form of rubai, a poem consisting of four lines with the rhyme of aaaa, aaba [3, p. 34]. According to the previous and latest researches, more than 300 Rubaiyat are ascribed to Mahsati Ganjavi [17, p. 157]. Mahsati Ganjavi wrote in Persian. In the 12th century, a lot of works were written in Persian not only in Azerbaijan, but also in the East, because that time Persian was the language of poetry. Such facts occurred throughout the history of literature of the world countries. Although the poets wrote in other languages, they benefited from the words, proverbs, expressions, oral folk literature of that nation [6, p. 446]. The purpose of the article is to bring together all the studies about Mahsati Ganjavi made by British orientalists from the beginning of the 20th century to the present time and to provide the essential details mentioned in these researches. The article uses the methods of manuscript and data analysis and comparative methods. The novelty of the article is to study all the researches about Mahsati Ganjavi made in the UK and give important information about the manuscript of the novel "Mahsati and Amir Ahmad" preserved in the British Library, as well as a bowl decorated with Mahsati Ganjavi's rubai in the Victoria and Albert Museum in London. Review of recent related publications. British studies about Mahsati Ganjavi. In British Orientalism, her name was first mentioned in the book, written by Edward Brown, the professor of Cambridge University. Edward Brown published a book "A Literary History of Persia" in 4 volumes. The book covers four periods of Persian literature. There is an information about Mahsati Ganjavi in the second volume of the book [3, p. 344]. It was told that the correct spelling of Mahsati's name is unknown. He noted that her name was pronounced like Mihisti, Mahasti and Mihasti and she wrote poems in the rubai genre. He described her famous story with Sultan Sanjar and added her rubai in English. For thee hath Heaven saddled Fortune's steed, O king and chosen thee from all who lead Now o'er the earth it spreads a silver sheet To guard from mud thy gold-shod charger's feet [3, p. 344]. He also noted that he was a mistress of Tajeddin Ahmad, the son of preacher of Ganja. In this book, Edward Brown mentioned that in "Tarikhi-Guzide" the following rubai attributed to Bintun Najjariya belonged to Mahsati Ganjavi [3, p. 345]. One cannot restrain me by hard words: one cannot keep me in the cheerless house: Her whose tresses are like chains one cannot keep at home [even'] with chains [4, p. 32]. I would like to note that the book written by Edward Brown is one of the most perfect works about the history of Persian literature. Edward Brown translated into English the 6th section of the 5th chapter which dealt with the lives of Persian poets in "Tarikhi Guzida" written by Hamdullah Qazvini in 1330 and published it in London in 1901. There is not much information about the poets here. Very brief information about Mahsati Ganjavi can be found in the "Biography of Prominent Women" (Itimadus Saltanas Khayrat Hisan) section. It was noted that the poetess had very beautiful quatrains. The etymology of the name Mahsati is also given (Mah means "big" and sati is "lady") and there are variants such as Mah-asti, Mih-asti. It was also noted that the literary exchange between Mahsati Ganjavi and Tajeddin Ahmad was amazing and he was married to Mahsati Ganjavi. The following rubai is given both in Persian and English. O idol mine, I will not suffer abasement at thy hands, Nor even at the hands of one who is superior to thee. I will not precipitately entangle my tresses in the noose I will lie at ease on the water and get not yet wet. In addition, two quatrains dedicated to the butcher boy were given in both Persian and English. It has been suggested that Mahsati fell in love with the butcher boy [4, p. 30]. Every knife which he withdraws from the victim he hath slain, and takes in his sugar-sweet lips and teeth. Were he to place it once again on the throat of the slain, it would renew its life for desire of its lips. The butcher, as is his custom, overthrew me, slew me, and said, "Such is my habit!" Again he treacherously lays his head on my feet, Breathing on me that he may flay me! [4, p. 30–31]. Mahsati's love poems to different boys made confusion and it was considered that she was in love with these boys. Among these young boys were butcher, cobbler, baker, a son of tailor, weaver, carpenter and so on. But actually all these poems dedicated to different craftsmen, men are shahrashubs, a genre in the poetry. The professor Rafael Huseynov, the author of the one of the prominent research dedicated to Mahsati Ganjavi, a prominent orientalist gave information about shahrashub genre in his book "Shahrashubs are poems or series of poems expressing cities, craftsmen and professionals" [15, p. 97]. He also mentioned that the terms shahrashub and shehrengiz are used in parallel in the literature [15, p. 92]. Information about the life and work of Mahsati Ganjavi is reflected in "Mahsati and Amir Ahmad", the romance of the 15th–16th centuries. The manuscript contains 4 copies. One of them is kept in the British Library, one in Istanbul University and the other two in the Institute of Manuscripts in Azerbaijan. The most complete version of this epos is a copy from the British Library. There is an article by Meredith Owens about the manuscript of the romance "Mahsati and Amir Ahmad" kept in the British Library. The article is called "A rare illustrated persian manuscript". Professor, turkologist, orientalist Glyn Munro Meredith Owens worked as a bibliographer at the British Library, and in the later years of his career he began working at the Department of Islamic Studies at the University of Toronto. Meredith Owens researched a collection of Persian and Turkish manuscripts collected at the British Museum. Among these manuscripts, he especially appreciated the manuscript of the romance "Mahsati and Amir Ahmad" which was about love affairs between Amir Ahmad, the son of the preacher and Mahsati Ganjavi the poetess in Ganja.

The article describes in detail the 12 miniatures in the manuscript or 8755. The manuscript was presented to the British Museum in 1917 by Darea Baroness Zouche. Previously, the manuscript is thought to have been in Turkey for a long time. The author came to this conclusion by analyzing the poems of Turkish origin in the manuscript, the explanations in the first folio 247 Література зарубіжних країн and the names of its previous owners. Preserved in the British Library or. 8755, this manuscript consists of 111 folios and was copied by the Nasta'liq line in 867/1462–1463, but it is not specified by whom it was copied. Another study of Mahsati Ganjavi in modern British oriental studies was conducted by Marle Hammond. In 2003, the first volume of the Encyclopedia of Women and Islamic Cultures featured an article by orientalist Marle Hammond entitled "Women Literature: 9th to 15th Century". Marle Hammond works in the Department of Near and Middle Eastern Languages and Cultures at the University of London and lectures on Arabic Literature and Culture. This article provides information on female writers who lived and created between the 9th and 15th centuries. The article also gives information about the history of that time. It is noted that the literature created by women has expanded in many places during this period of Islamic history. However, the literature created by women was not isolated from men's literature. Thus, most of the literary works were mainly included into the collections of male poets. This period of Islamic history is characterized by political centralization and ethnic, linguistic and cultural pluralism. Thus, the period falls between the Abbasid Caliphate's coming to the power in 132/750 overthrowing the Umayyads and conquering Constantinople by the Ottoman

Empire in 857/1453. The gradual weakening of the central government in Baghdad has led to the emergence of more localised seat of power, many of them competing each other in their patronage of art. As a result, the period was characterized by the development of the Arabian prose, the rise of Persian poetry, the golden age of Hebrew literature and the emergence of Romance. At the beginning of this period, Arabic was the leading vehicle for Islamic literary culture. However, in the middle of this period, during the rule of the Samanids (819–1005) and Ghaznavids (977– 1186), Persian became the favourite language in the palaces. During this period, it was written only in these two languages, but it is assumed that there are examples of women's literature in other languages that existed in the Islamic Empire in this period. After a brief commentary on the history of Islamic literature, it is shown that some women writers, as well as Mahsati Ganjavi, are being talked about. It is further noted that Mahsati Ganjavi ranks among the pioneers of Persian rubai. It is also shown that Mahsati wrote poems in the genre of shahrashub and Farid ad-din Attar (1220) in his "Ilahiname" referred to Mahsati as "Debir" (the scribe). It is also stated in the article that Attar's "Ilahiname" contains information about two legendary women, Mahsati Ganjavi and Rabia al-Adawiyya. Then there is another interesting issue about carving women's poems on some objects. Of course, these items has played an important role in studying women poetry, as well as their social, political and cultural positions in history. It is mentioned that there is a ceramic bowl kept in the Victoria and Albert Museum in London whose exterior was decorated with a rubai which ascribes to Mahsati. Of course, the text may be short and of limited value to researchers, but they can tell us much about female poetry patterns, their history, location and status. In the article "Mahsati Ganjavi et les potiers de Rey", Firuz Bagirzadeh investigated archaeological, textual, historical, artistic and religious-political evidences to identify the possible source of rubai on the aforementioned ceramic bowl. Bagirzade noted that this poem might belong to both Mahsati and Seljuk panegyrist Anwari (1190). Taking into account the history of the bowl and the variation in color, the author stated that the origin of the bowl dated back to 1155 and 1223, as well as its location is Iraq. Then, taking into account the geopolitical and social history of the region, Bagirzadeh came to the conclusion that the poem belonges more to Mahsati than to Anvari. Anwari could not gain popularity in Iraqi-Ajam at that time because of the fact that Anwari belonged to the Sunni sect and Iraqi-Ajam was dominated by Shi'i sects when sectarianism prevailed in that region during that period. Also, Mahsati's relationship with masters and artists can be assumed that the poetess was a favorite for Haft-color artists. This bowl is no small indication for a poetess whose career has been overshadowed by the legends. It also emphasizes the importance of Mahsati Ganjavi not only for aristocratic society, but also as a poetess among the merchantile classes. One of the studies made by British Orientalists was in the book of "Borrowed ware" written by Dick Davis. In this book, there is some information about Mahsati Ganjavi. He mentioned that Mahsati Ganjavi was born in Ganja and was a scribe at the court of the Seljuk monarch Sanjar (1119–1157). The author is also told that the Safavid poets of the 16th century particularly admired her and added the translation of some her quatrains. Dear, dry your pointless tears, tears don't suit you – I'm sad enough, you needn't be sad too; Look, you're the loved one, crying's not your role – Let me do what the lover has to do [2]. In 2013, the BBC Radio broadcasted a program called "The Golden Age of Islam". Topics about prominent thinkers and their achievements were heard here. The program covered the period from the eighth to the thirteenth centuries, and featured 20 programs about invention, medicine, mathematics, literature and philosophy. One of these programs was about two outstanding women poets – Rabiah Balkhi and Mahsati Ganjavi. This section was presented by Nargiz Ferzad, the Persian Speaker of SOAS (School of African and Oriental Studies). First, information was given about the tragic life of Rabia Balkhi. The beautiful Rabia Balkhi, who came out of the palace, lived in Afghanistan and wrote poems about love and beauty from her youth. As for Mahsati Ganjavi, Nargez Farzad told about her life. She was born in Ganja, and wrote rubai. She was a poetess in the palace of Sultan Mahmud (1118–1131) and his uncle Sultan Sanjar (1131–1157). Mahsati Ganjavi was famous in the Seljuk palace. In addition, that Mahsati was reportedly imprisoned for insulting the king twice. It was mentioned that little is known about Mahsati's early life. It was also noted that her father gave her a good education, and at the age of 19, Mahsati was a good musician and played well on lute and harp. It is said that Mahsati was married to the son of preacher of Ganjai, and Amir Ahmad was also a poet. Mahsati Ganjavi's quatrains expressed the love and optimism. Nargiz Farzad recited some of Mahsati Ganjavi's rubaiyat in Persian and English. Those nights when I slept softly in your arms, have gone, All the pearls I polished by my lashes, have gone. You were born for my soul, a loved companion, you left me and all that I shared with you, have gone.

Conclusions. It is an important event for comparative literature studies to translate the works of Azerbaijani literature into English. First of all, translating such kind of couregous poetry into English plays a great role in recognition and studying Azerbaijan Classical literature not only in the UK but also in the world. The studies by the British Orientalists led to the recognition of Mahsati Ganjavi, as well as her involvement in scientific analysis. First of all, her gender makes Mahsati Ganjavi an extraordinary figure in the world literature. Because that time only male poets wrote about love. That's why Mahsati Ganjavi's poetry caused a lot debates. The Preservation of Mahsati Ganjavi's manuscript in the British Library, as well as the discovery of a bowl decorated with Mahsati Ganjavi's rubai in the Victoria and Albert Museum in London, are very important to study Mahsati Ganjavi's heritage deeply.

References: 1. Rousseau A. Parnasse Oriental. Alger, 1841. 207 p. 2. Davis D. Borrowed Ware: Medieval Persian Epigrams. London, 1996. 212 p. 3. Browne E. G. A literary history of Persia : in 4 vol. Cambridge, 1956. Vol. 2 : From Firdawsi to Sadi. 568 p. 4. Hamd Allah Mustawfi Qazvini, Browne E. G. Biographies of the Persian Poets from the Tarikh-I-Guzida. Whitefish : Kessinger Publishing, 1901. 76 p. 5. Meier F. Die schöne Mahsati. Ein beitrag zur geschichte des persischen viezeilers. Wiesbaden, 1963. 412 S. 6. Gibb E.J.W. A History of Ottoman Empire.

Volume 1. London, 1900. 447 p. 7. Hammond M. Women Literature: 9th to 15th century. Encyclopedia of Women and Islamic Cultures / ed. J. Suad. Leiden : Brill, 2011. Vol. 1 : Methodologies, Paradigms and Sources. P. 42–50. 8. Owens M. A rare illustrated Persian manuscript "Amir Ahmad u Mahsati". British Library Research on the Art of Asia, 9 September 1901 – 30 September 1964 / O. Aslanapa, R. Naumann. Istanbul : Baha Matbaasi, 1969. P. 172–181. 9. A statue of Mahsati Ganjavi is erected in the French city of Cognac. 10. Smith P. Rubaiyat of Mahsati. London : New Humanity Books, 2013. 198 p. 11. Smith P. The Rubai (Quatrain) in Sufi Poetry: An Anthology. London : New Humanity Books, 2012. 475 p. 12. Sprachman P. Suppressed Persian: An anthology of Forbidden Literature. California, 1995. 111 p. 13. Hüseynov R. Söz tək qəzəl Məhsəti. Bakı : Şərq-Qərb, 2013. 560 s. 14. Hüseynov R. Məhsəti Gəncəvi – özü, sözü, izi ilə. Bakı : Nurlan, 2005. 560 s. 15. Hüseynov R. Məhsəti Gəncəvi. Portret-oçerk (20 dilə tərcümə olunmuş kitab). Bakı : Şərq-Qərb, 2013. 128 s. 16. Gould R. Mahsati of Ganja's Wandering Quatrains: Translator's Introduction. Literary Imagination. 2011. Vol. 13. № 2. P. 225–227. 17. Sharma S. Wandering Quatrains and Woman Poets. The Treasury of Tabriz: The Great Il-Khanid Compendium / eds. A. A. Seyed-Gohrab, S. McGlinn. Amsterdam : Rozenburg Publishers, 2007. P. 153–170. 249 Література зарубіжних країн Маммедова Ілаха Салахаддін гизи. МАХС

Miniatures from
The Courtesan and the Preacher:
The Romance of Mahsati,
an Early Female Persian Poet
British Library Manuscript, Turkoman Style Or. 8755

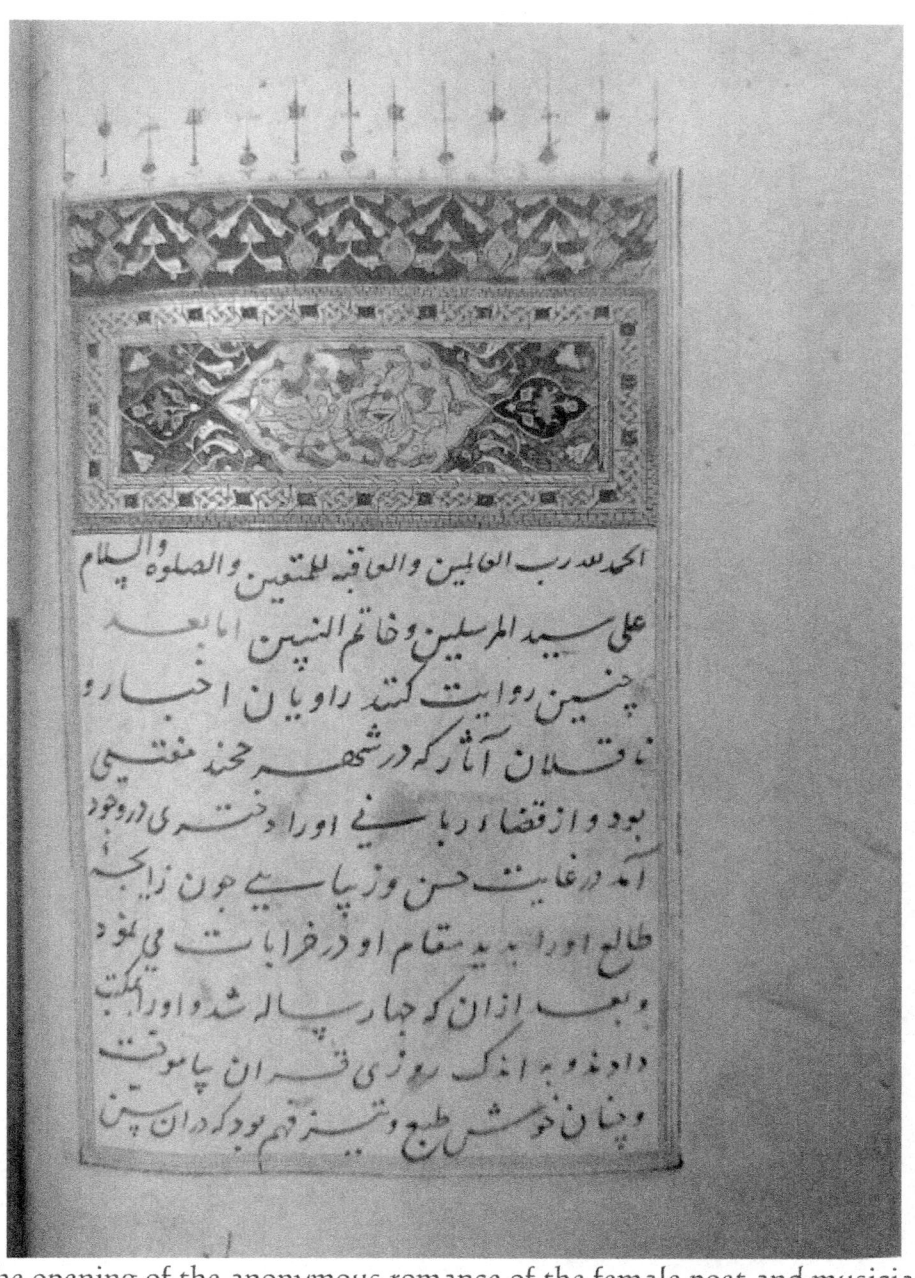

الحمد لله رب العالمين والعاقبة للمتقين والصلوة والسلام
على سيد المرسلين و خاتم النبيين اما بعد
چنین روایت کنند راویان اخبار و
ناقلان آثار که در شهر گنجه محمد مفتیی
بود و از قضا در با سینی او را دختری در وجود
آمد در غایت حسن و زیبایی چون زاچه
طالع او را بدید مقام او در خرابات مینمود
و بعد از آنکه چهار ساله شد او را مکتب
دادند و به اندک روزی قرآن را ختم کرد
و بنان خوش طبع و تیز فهم بود که در آن سنین

The opening of the anonymous romance of the female poet and musician Mahsati and Amir Ahmad the preacher's son. Copy dated Rabi' I 867/1462 (British Library Or.8755, f. 22v)

Mahsati and Amir Ahmad see each other for the first time (British Library Or.8755, f. 29v)

The mule leads Amir Ahmad back to Mahsati (British Library Or.8755, f. 70r)

نزد خطیب کنجه برند تا حال ویرا بهین منوال بہ پند رساند
گفت بر عثمان نمی تواند برخاستن امیر احمد گفت ویرا بدوش
برگیرید و بسوی بنهان کردند و پیر را دوش خوش

A drunken Pir 'Usman is carried home (British Library Or.8755, f. 75v)

Mahsati entertaining the poets of Khurasan (British Library Or.8755, f. 87r)

Amir Ahmad and Mahsati accosted by a drunkard in the bazaar (British Library Or.8755, f. 95v)

The great Azerbaijani poetess Mahsati Ganjavi, who lived in the late 11th and early 12th centuries, is a brilliant representative of the Azerbaijani and Muslim renaissance and a representative of the poetry of the new city. She is the first famous Azerbaijani poet, the first female chess player, the first prominent female musician and, most likely, the first female composer.

The date of the poet's birth is given in the epos 'Amir Ahmad and Mahsati'. Mahsati Ganjavi was born in about 1089 in Ganja and lived there until the end of her life. Her real name was Manija, and she took the name Mahsati as a literary pseudonym.

For some time, Mahsati lived in the palace of the great Sultan Sanjar, attended his receptions and literary meetings held here. It is said that she was closely involved in the palace life of Sultan Muhammad and his son Sultan Mahmud.

Information about the life of the great poet is mainly taken from the 13th century epic 'Mahsati and Amir Ahmad' kept at the Azerbaijan Institute of Manuscripts, Istanbul and London.

The summary of the saga is as follows: She is the daughter of a theologian living in Balkh. He turns to astrologers to find out the child's fate. The stars indicate that the girl will have a great future and will win the competition and love of the people. However, it is said that the girl's fate will be connected with the ruin (drinking place, tavern). The father sends his daughter to school. Mahsati is well educated until the age of eighteen.

Then Mahsati studies 12 mughams and 24 of them. She also learned to play the harp, the *oud*, and other instruments from musicians. The people are amazed and ask her father: 'How is this possible? Do you first educate your daughter well, teach her the Qur'an, and then prepare her for dancing?" The father answers that if she has ruin on her forehead, let her be ready for it. After the death of her father, Mahsati moved to Ganja and lived in a neighbourhood called Kharabat.

Amir Ahmad and Mahsati, the only son of the Ganja preacher, fall in love. At the request of the Shah of Ganja, the poet moved to the palace once and for all, Mahsati Amir offered Ahmad to flee to Balkh. First, the poetess goes there herself. Poets of Balkh and all of Khorasan gather here in honor of his arrival, and a poetry contest begins. Mahsati tells a poetic riddle. No one can open it. At this point in the race, a stranger appears and tells the answer to the riddle in a beautiful poem. Everyone understands that the person in front of them is Amir Ahmad. At the end of the saga, it is stated that the lovers return to their native Ganja, officially conclude their marriage, and from this marriage they have two children.

After the death of his father, Amir Ahmad became the preacher of Ganja. Then he goes to mercy himself. Mahsati sheds so many tears over the death of Amir Ahmad that in the end his eyes are closed. The poetess can live two years after her lover.

The saga shows that Mahsati was buried next to Nizami Ganjavi. Indeed, in 1923, when Nizami's tomb was exhumed for burial in the Shah Abbas Mosque, the body of a woman was found next to him. One of Nizami's poems proves their acquaintance. It is believed that these verses are dedicated to Mahsati:

If your art is to play music,
I want to hear bells and bells
Do not pull the lashes sideways
Horse an arrow, roast
You know I can't live without you,
If you want my life, take it, I'll give it to you.
I see, in vain I hoped for success,
I call you with my last breath.
Nizami gives his life for you -
Accept, as I accept suffering ...

For the first time, Sahab Tahiri collected *ruba'is, qit'as* and *ghazals* of Mahsati from various sources, and in 1957, he composed a *divan* consisting of about 200 poems.

Mahsati Ganjavi's *ruba'is* have been translated not only into Azerbaijani, but also into English, Italian, German and French. A museum of Mahsati Ganjavi was established in Ganja and a statue was erected in 1980.

The dominant literature in Azerbaijan in the 12th century was palace literature. Palace poets lived in Shirvan and Tabriz in the palace of Shirvanshahs and also Eldegiz, and served to increase their respect and prestige. However, the poets who defended the interests of the city's artists and the urban poor lived outside the palace, and there was a serious struggle between these two literary currents. Nizami Ganjavi was a genius poet who expressed the needs and desires of urban artisans, urban and rural poor on a large scale during this period. Among the great contemporary poets of Nizami, Mahsati Ganjavi was one of the poets who was close to the people with his democratic views and expressed the mood of the city's artists.

Mahsati Ganjavi, one of the founders of the school of poetry in Azerbaijani literature in the 12th century, whose real name is thought to be Manija, is one of the artists who played an important role in the emergence and development of humanism in literature. Little is known about the life of Mahsati, who was born and raised in Ganja. Ancient commentators reported that this talented poetess was born and raised in a poor family, was a good musicologist, had a conflict with the son of the Ganja preacher Amir Ahmad, and was exiled from Ganja. In all the various information about Mahsati, it is clear that she was an extremely talented poet of his time and gained high prestige and respect among the people. Mahsati's image also attracted the attention of a number of writers.

The author of 'Sword and Pen' Ordubadi, Dilbazi and others tried to create an artistic copy of Mahsati Ganjavi. Mahsati Ganjavi's well-known *ruba'is* in the Middle East are not fully available. Just as the manuscripts of this famous artist have not survived to our day, very few of the *ruba'i* have survived. Along with *ruba'is*, the poet also wrote *qit'as* and *ghazals*. The face of her works was copied and the *divan* was closed, but later this *divan* disappeared and has not survived to the present day. Her *ruba'is* have been collected from various historical and literary sources and from the epos 'Amir Ahmad and Mahsati'.

THE LATEST NEWS ON MAHSATI

UNESCO MARKS 900th ANNIVERSARY OF AZERBAIJANI POETESS MAHSATI GANJAVI

Sat 18 May 2013

Elchin Efendiyev spoke of the creativity of Mahsati Ganjavi.

The United Nations Educational, Scientific and Cultural Organization (UNESCO) with the organizational support of Azerbaijan`s permanent representation at this organization and the Ministry of Culture and Tourism of Azerbaijan have marked the 900th anniversary of the Azerbaijani poetess Mahsati

Ganjavi (12th century). Deputy Prime Minister of Azerbaijan Elchin Efendiyev spoke of the creativity of Mahsati Ganjavi, noting, that as the world coryphaei Dante, Rabelais, Fizuli, Shakespeare, Cervantes, Voltaire and Tolstoy, the Azerbaijani poetess Mahsati belongs to the entire humanity, with her literary heritage, AzerTAc reports. "Not by chance that President of Azerbaijan has issued a special decree on celebration of Mahsati Ganjavi`s 900th anniversary", Efendiyev underlined. "Such respect for national literary heritage was established still by the late national leader of Azerbaijan Heydar Aliyev", he said. Elchin Efendiyev stressed the role of Azerbaijan`s First Lady, UNESCO Goodwill Ambassador Mehriban Aliyeva in development of bilateral relations between Azerbaijan and UNESCO.

The ceremony was addressed by Dr. Tang Qian, UNESCO Assistant Director-General for Education, Azerbaijani MP, correspondent member of Azerbaijan National Academy of Sciences, the researcher of Mahsati Ganjav's creativity Rafael Huseynov. Rafael Huseynov in particular said: "Mahsati Ganjavi was a 12th century poet, born in Ganja, Azerbaijan. She received education, closely acquainted with Eastern literature and music. Mahsati Ganjavi was a famous *ruba'i* writer recognized not only in her epoch, but much later also. Her most productive period of creation was spent in the palace of Sultan Mahmud Seljuk and that of his uncle Sanjar Seljuk. Mahsati Ganjavi commonly wrote *ruba'i* in Persian. The love plot holds the main place in her creations.

The *ruba'is* are marked out by their worldliness, humanism, epicurism and optimism. Mahsati Ganjavi describes love as a fragile natural feeling, which makes a ma's fame higher. The poetess protested against religious prejudices, hypocrisy and conservatism, and protected a man's moral freedom. Her poems reflected the people's, especially, the women`s romantic dreams of a free and happy life."

The event culminated with a concert of Azerbaijani masters of art.

Mahsati Ganjavi Centre in Ganjeh

The Mahsati Ganjavi Centre was built with the support of the Heydar Aliyev Foundation. On January 21, 2014, President of Azerbaijan Ilham Aliyev attended the inauguration of the centre.

The centre accommodates an art gallery devoted to the poetess's creativity, a reading room for researchers, a music studio, a music notes library, and mugham, piano sections and other auxiliary rooms.

The reading room has been provided with books about the life and creativity of Mahsati Ganjavi, her literary legacy, rubáiyáts of the poetess in Azerbaijani, Russian and English in an electronic format, along with publications of Azerbaijan's eminent poets and thinkers, and about Azerbaijani music and carpet-making.

Photos from the exhibitions and concerts held in connection with the 900th jubilee of Mahsati Ganjaviwith the organizational support of the Heydar Aliyev Foundationin the cities of Reims and Melouse of France in November and December last year, as well as national music instruments are exhibited at the centre.

In a national garments exhibition of the Centre, national garments related to the Mahsati time, in particular, those of ladies of the Renaissance Period are exhibited, and in an art gallery, various displays devoted to Mahsati Ganjavi image and her rubáiyáts, as well as samples of art and monumental works are presented. A monument to the poetess has been erected in the Mahsati room. Miniatures and art works are presented hereusing a projector.

A park has been laid out around the centre.

About 70 rare manuscripts of Mahsati Ganjavi to be brought to Azerbaijan from abroad next week

01.04.2013

Ganja, April 1 (AzerTAc). About 70 rare manuscripts of Mahsati Ganjavi kept in different libraries around the world will be brought to Azerbaijan next week, deputy director for scientific affairs at Ganja Scientific Center of the National Academy of Sciences Samir Pishnamazzade has said. He said about 70 miniatures, illustrations and quatrains of Mahsati Ganjavi kept in Egypt`s Library of Alexandria, Metropolitan Museum of Art and Yale University in the United States will be brought by Nizami Ganjavi International Center. Manuscripts date back to the 14th – 15th centuries, he added.

Pishnamazzade said about 100 illustrations of Mahsati Ganjavi are being kept in various libraries of the world. "Six monographies dedicated to Mahsati Ganjavi by famous English researcher Paul Smith were brought to the country on her 900th anniversary. Currently they are being translated."

Conference on Mahsati Ganjavi takes place in French Mulhouse

23 JUNE 2014

A conference devoted to the 900th jubilee of Azerbaijan's first poetess Mahsati Ganjavi was held at the Upper Alsace University in the city of Mulhouse, France, the Heydar Aliyev Foundation reported.

The conference with the theme of "A universal bridge linking the 12th and 21st centuries: Mahsati Ganjavi, a philosopher, writer and poetess of the Oriental Renaissance (12th century)" was held with the support of the Heydar Aliyev Foundation and Azerbaijan's Embassy in France at the department of literature, languages and humanitarian sciences of the Upper Alsace University in the city of Mulhouse.

Dean of the department, Greta Komur-Thilloy noted that Mahsati Ganjavi has been known to the Eastern world not only as a poetess, but also a philosopher, chess player and musician. He added that her works personify a pure and free love and freedom of woman.

Komur-Thilloy underscored that naming the hall, in which the conference took place, after Mahsati Ganjavi was another contribution to the cooperation between the two countries. He said, due to efforts by the Heydar Aliyev Foundation, this cooperation has developed further.

The University's Rector Christine Gangloff-Ziegler said Mahsati Ganjavi's legacy has shown high values, ancient and rich literature of Azerbaijan.

Gangloff-Ziegler noted interest in creating a department associated with Azerbaijan's literature and culture at the university. The rector said even she herself has started to learn the Azerbaijani language.

She thanked the Heydar Aliyev Foundation for the support provided to create the Mahsati Ganjavi Hall.

Addressing the conference, Azerbaijan's Ambassador to France Elchin Amirbeyov described Mahsati Ganjavi as a shining star of the Eastern world. He mentioned a special event was held at

UNESCO and several other conferences held in a number of countries devoted to the poetess.

Talking about the relations between Azerbaijan and France, Amirbeyov underscored significant projects implemented following the initiative of President of the Heydar Aliyev Foundation, Azerbaijan's First Lady Mehriban Aliyeva aimed at promoting Azerbaijan's cultural treasures in France - a cradle of the world culture.

Speeches were also made by Chairperson of the Ganja Department of the Azerbaijan Writers Union Mammad Alim, Employee of the French International Academy of Diplomacy, Scholar-orientalist Shirin Melikova, Director of the Manuscripts Institute under the Azerbaijan National Academy of Sciences named after Fuzuli, corresponding member of the Academy Teymour Kerimli, and Teacher of the Azerbaijani language at the French State Oriental Languages and Cultures Institute (INALCO) Aygun Eyyubova.

Moreover, within the framework of the conference, a Protocol of Understanding for cooperation was signed between the Upper Alsace University and the Ganja State University.

After the conference, the hall named after Mahsati Ganjavi at the Upper Alsace University's literature, languages and humanitarian sciences was inaugurated.

Following, Dean of the Department Greta Komur-Thilloy, City Mayor Jean Rotner, Rector of the University Christine Gangloff-Ziegler, Senator Jean-Marie Bockel and Azerbaijan's Ambassador to France Elchin Amirbeyov delivered a speech.

They emphasized the hall's restoration by the Heydar Aliyev Foundation and underscored the significant contribution made by the foundation to the cooperation between the two countries.

Books printed by the Heydar Aliyev Foundation on the life and creativity of Mahsati Ganjavi were also put on display in the hall.

At the end of the event, masters of art performed classic works of Azerbaijani and European composers.

A number of cultural events, including exhibitions and concerts were recently held as part of the 900th anniversary of Azerbaijan's first poetess and chess player with the support of the Heydar Aliyev Foundation in France.

Mahsati Ganjavi is considered a bright representative of the Muslim Orient.

Mahsati Ganjavi. Portrait-essay.

Huseynov Rafael

Baku, 2013, Publishing House "Sharq-Qarb",

120 pages.

Rafael Huseynov

MAHSATI GANJAVI

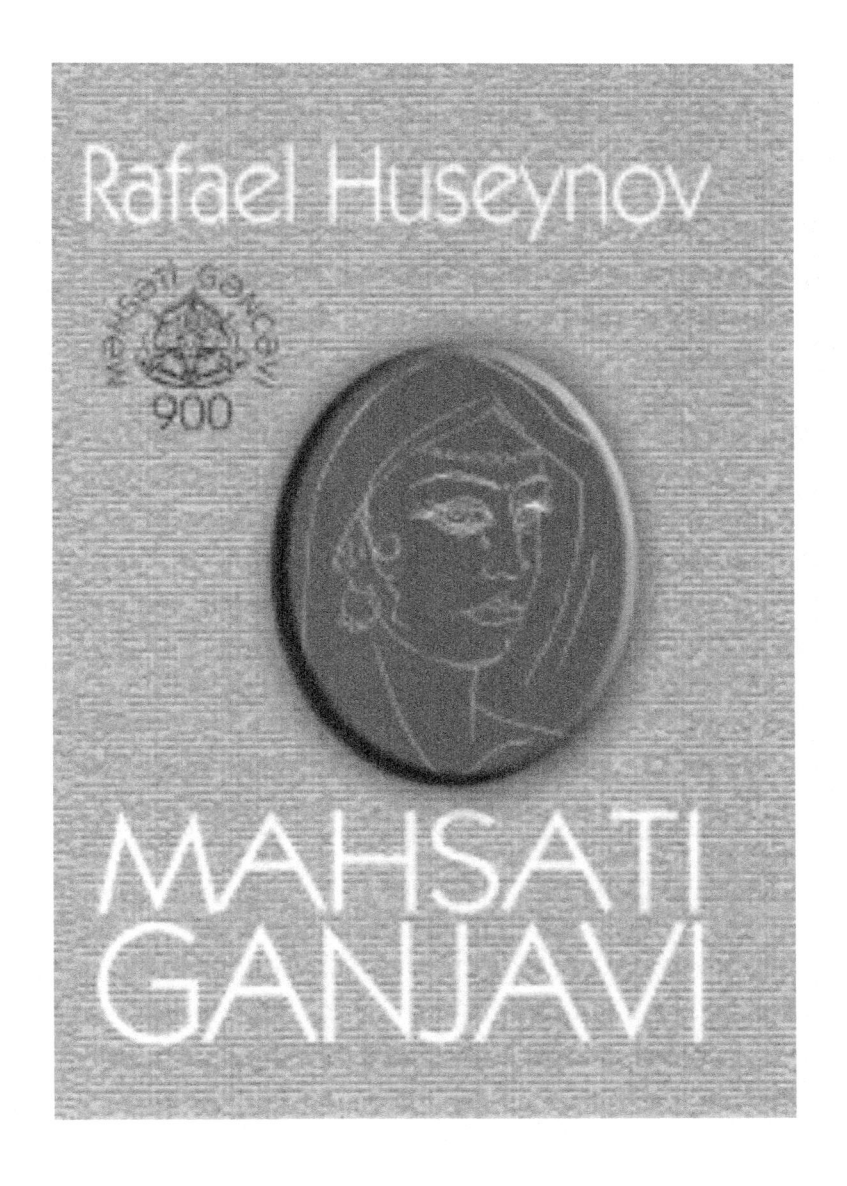

Great Azerbaijani poetess Mahsati Ganjavi gained popularity not only as an unprecedented word-master but also as a skillful musician and chess-player. Mahsati khanym who was born 900 years ago in ancient city of Ganja has been known as the most superior writer of rubai for all times in the poetry of the nations of Near and Middle East along with her contemporary Omar

Khayyam. Including certain historical sources, the genius Azerbaijani poet Nizami Ganjavi and the prominent sufi Faridaddin Attar have written about Mahsati as an owner of the big influence in literary and cultural atmosphere still in 12th century. Mahsati Ganjavi has praised pure love and humanist ideals in her rubais thus being perceived as one of the most courageous representatives of freethinking in poetry and has strongly influenced the further progress of the Oriental literature. Portrait-essay pursues the way of life covered by Mahsati Ganjavi, her literary heritage and the major features of her literary activities, as well as investigates the main credits of the mighty poetess in the progress history of the word of art.

2013 Azerbaijani stamp of the Persian poet Mahsati

Mahsati Ganjavi Museum in Ganja

An exhibition and a concert devoted to Mahsati Ganjavi in Reims

In November 2013, an exhibition and a concert devoted to the 900th jubilee of Azerbaijani poetess Mahsati Ganjavi was organized in the French city of Reims, with organizational support from the Heydar Aliyev Foundation and assistance by the country's Embassy in France.

At an exhibition organized on November 28 at the Tau Palace of the city of Reims, garments related to Mahsati Ganjavi's time, carpets with illustrations drawn to the poetess's works, ancient coins, samples of coppersmithery and pottery art, china dishes and other exhibits were displayed. At a concert organized on November 30 at the Reims Conservatoire, along with works by Uzeir Hajibeyli, Tofig Gouliyev, Fikret Amirov, Shafiga Akhundova and other composers, also popular songs and pieces of music composed to lyrics by Mahsati Ganjavi were performed, and rubaiyats of the poetess translated into the French languages were read. After the concert, books with Mahsati Ganjavi's rubaiyats in English and French translations were distributed to the audience.

France holds exhibition marking 900th anniversary of great Azerbaijani poetess Mahsati Ganjavi

The Heydar Aliyev Foundation and Azerbaijani embassy in France organized an exhibition marking the 900th anniversary of Azerbaijani poetess Mahsati Ganjavi in the Palace of Tau in Reims, France, SIA reports citing AzerTAC. Opening the exhibition, administrator of the palace Benua-Anri Papuno said such events have an exceptional role in helping people belonging to various cultures to get to know each other better. He said the exhibits showcased point to ancient and rich culture of Azerbaijan. In turn, Deputy Mayor of Reims Jacques Quen said he was pleased that Azerbaijan participates in an international fair in Reims for the first time, adding that Azerbaijani artists would perform in Reims Conservatoire as part of a series of events celebrating Ganjavi's anniversary. Noting that Azerbaijan is rich in cultural values, Quen said he was confident that the exhibits displayed here would get the people in this city to see Azerbaijan as an ancient country. Jean-Paul Bashi, chairman of the Regional Council of Champagne-Ardenne, said he visited Azerbaijan as part of a French delegation a few weeks ago to attend the 3rd World Humanitarian Forum. He said

Azerbaijan is located at the intersection of two continents, on border with Muslim countries and at the crossroads of civilizations. Emphasizing that Azerbaijan is rich in natural resources, particularly, oil and gas, he added that Baku and Ganja are largest cities of the country and both have acquired modern look lately. He noted Reims University is interested in building ties with Ganja State University. Recalling that he participated in a wine festival in Ganja, Jean-Paul Bashi said Champagne-Ardenne is known for its wines worldwide, and that they attach importance to cooperation with Ganja in this area. He underlined growing tourism potential of Azerbaijan and a need to build ties in this field, too. He said Mahsati Ganjavi is not only known for rubais (quatrains) where she glorifies the beauties of her homeland, but also as a singer of lyric love songs.

Counselor of the Azerbaijani embassy in France Nigar Huseynova said Mahsati Ganjavi, who was the 12th century poetess, writer, artist and master of calligraphy, was born and created her works in Ganja, one of the culture centers of East Renaissance. She said Ganjavi's works are marked out by their worldliness, humanity and optimism and that her ideas are still relevant though 900 years have passed. Huseynova said schools and streets are named after Ganjavi in Azerbaijan, a monument to her was built in her hometown in 1980. She added President Ilham Aliyev signed a decree on her 900th anniversary, her rubais were translated into various languages upon the initiative of President of Heydar Aliyev Foundation Mehriban Aliyeva and that she has also been commemorated by UNESCO. Ganja Mayor Elmar Valiyev said being second largest city of Azerbaijan, Ganja is also an ancient center of art and culture and great writers like Nizami Ganjavi and Mahsati Ganjavi originated from this city. He said he was proud that 870th anniversary of Nizami Ganjavi and 900th anniversary of Mahsati Ganjavi are marked in Azerbaijan and abroad under the presidential decree. He noted that Ganja was announced Capital of European Youth 2016. Valiyev said Heydar Aliyev Foundation led by First Lady Mehriban Aliyeva implements significant projects to promote cultural values of Azerbaijan in France and that a ceremonial event about Azerbaijan which also involved the First lady was held in Reims last year. Vice-President of Reims University, Professor Nuraddin Manamanni said they were interested in building ties with Ganja State University, including bilateral cooperation and exchange of students. Women's clothing dating back to the period of Mahsati Ganjavi, carpets reflecting illustrations of the poetess` works, samples of old coins, pieces of copper and pottery works, porcelain and other exhibits caused great interest among the visitors.

900

Məhsəti Gəncəvi
yaradıcılığı

182

OPEN CENTRAL ASIA BOOK FORUM & LITERATURE FESTIVAL 2013
DEDICATED TO 900 YEARS ANNIVERSARY OF MAHSATI GANJAVI

Baku, Ganja. Azerbaijan
3rd - 5th MAY
2013

Organising committee head office:
Suite 125, 43 Bedford Street Covent Garden London WC2E 9HA, UK
Tel.: +44 777 613 44 03,
E-mail: silkroadmedia.books@ocamagazine.com
www.ocabookforum.com, www.hertfordshirepress.com

HERTFORDSHIRE PRESS

EST. 2002
Silk Road Media

"To penetrate into the essence of all being and significance
and to release the fragrance of that inner attainment
for the guidance and benefit of others, by expressing
in the world of forms, truth, love, purity and beauty...
this is the only game which has any intrinsic and absolute
worth. All other, happenings, incidents and attainments can,
in themselves, have no lasting importance."
Meher Baba

Printed in Great Britain
by Amazon